The Grief Journey When a Child Dies

The Road We Travel

KELLY KLECKNER

&

JOANN SMITH

Copyright © 2024, 2025 Kelly Kleckner, LLC
All rights reserved.
ISBN: 978-1-960252-02-9

No part of this book may be reproduced or transmitted in any form or by any means, electronic or mechanical, including photocopying, recording or by any information storage and retrieval system, without written permission from Kelly Kleckner, LLC.

DEDICATION

From Kelly:
To my children, Diego, Carina, Jocelyn, and Mariana. To all my friends, family and co-workers that have been here for me on this grief journey. To all bereaved parents, grandparents, and siblings of a child of any age that has died too soon, you are not alone.

From JoAnn:
Dedicated first and foremost to John, my husband, best friend, Brian's father, and my strongest pillar of support. To our children, Molly, Mike and Heather and their spouses. To my family and friends who continue to walk with us on our grief journey. Your support and willingness to remember Brian will always be deeply appreciated.

To all who are living with and through the loss of a child or grandchild, may Brian's story and how our family traveled this road provide some hope and encouragement as you navigate through your own unique journey.

 LOVE IS FOREVER

CONTENTS

1	Introduction	1
2	The Beginning	5
3	The Week Before	13
4	The Day Between Before & After	19
5	The Day Spider-Man 2 was Released	25
6	After...	33
7	Ruby/Max/Mia	47
8	Dreams & Feelings	53
9	Helping Others Helps Me	61

CONTENTS

Brian

10 **March 15th, 2008**   65
11 **Courage**   77
12 **Moving from Grief to Gratitude with Pilates**   87
13 **My Faith Journey**   93
14 **Be the Keeper of Their Story**   99
15 **Meeting Our Needs when Grieving**   107
16 **Memories - Shared by Loved Ones**   113
17 **Remembering Our Children**   143
18 **Finding Your Grief Support**   151
19 **For Our Supporters**   157

About the Authors   163

CHAPTER 1
INTRODUCTION

Thank you for taking the time to read this book. Whether you are a family member, friend, whether we have never met yet or will never meet, the stories and content in this book are written with the deepest love that JoAnn and I have for our sons that have gone too soon. We are grateful that we can share them and this book with you.

I am taking a moment to write this introduction today on the 20th Anniversary of my son's death, June 26, 2024. I wanted this book to be published today but things don't always go according to plan, do they? Any of us grieving the death of our child, grandchild, sibling, or another loved one know this so well. We never would have planned this in a million years. It did not go according to our plan at all.

For many people, today is just another date on the calendar, but for me it is the date that is etched in my memory forever. JUNE 26th. Every June 26th, it will be the same, the date that changed my life forever.

Time just keeps moving on and year after year it gets further and further into the future without my son here. Each June 26th can feel different, some years I cried a bunch, other years I felt numb and tired, other years it might be a combo of those feelings. I do not always know how I will feel when the day comes here each year. I have learned to allow myself to feel how I need to feel that day and in that moment. I will say, however, that over time the intensity of the feelings has softened and is not as harsh as it was in the beginning. It does not mean I feel less love for my son; it means that now when thinking about him I remember him with a smile and the beautiful memories, not just memories of the "death story" and him not being here.

Each year I go to the cemetery with my daughters where I made a tradition of taking a picture of them by their brother's gravestone and I also take one of me at his gravestone. Then after that I decide what I will do. Today, we went and ate together at a restaurant. Some years I do not feel up to that. I do not know what the difference is, but I just go with the flow of it. I remember one year going to the store after, another year we got food to go and ate at home, and I am sure some years I just went home and laid in bed.

THE GRIEF JOURNEY WHEN A CHILD DIES

Today after going to the cemetery and eating, I watched tv for a bit and then took a nap. I felt so worn out. Then I spent the evening with my granddaughter and daughters.

Every JUNE 26th can be different and that is ok. What you choose to do on certain days is your choice, just do not hurt yourself, others, or the environment. You choose what you will do. We are on a grief journey and that is ok. We need to feel our feelings! We loved them so much and where there is great love, there is grief.

*For those of you reading this because you personally know JoAnn or myself, thank you for taking the time to read our stories. We appreciate it and love it when you remember our sons.

*For those of you that are reading this book and do not personally know us, thank you for taking the time to read our stories and getting to know our sons, Diego, and Brian.

*If you are a bereaved parent, grandparent or sibling of a child that has died of any age know that you are not alone. JoAnn and I are sharing our stories and other content in this book as a way of supporting you on your grief journey. All our grief journeys are different, yet we are not alone.

If you enjoy this book, feel free to share a review on Amazon or share with a friend or family member that may benefit from reading this book. Thank you!

Introduction written by:
Diego's Mom, Kelly

THE GRIEF JOURNEY WHEN A CHILD DIES

CHAPTER 2
THE BEGINNING

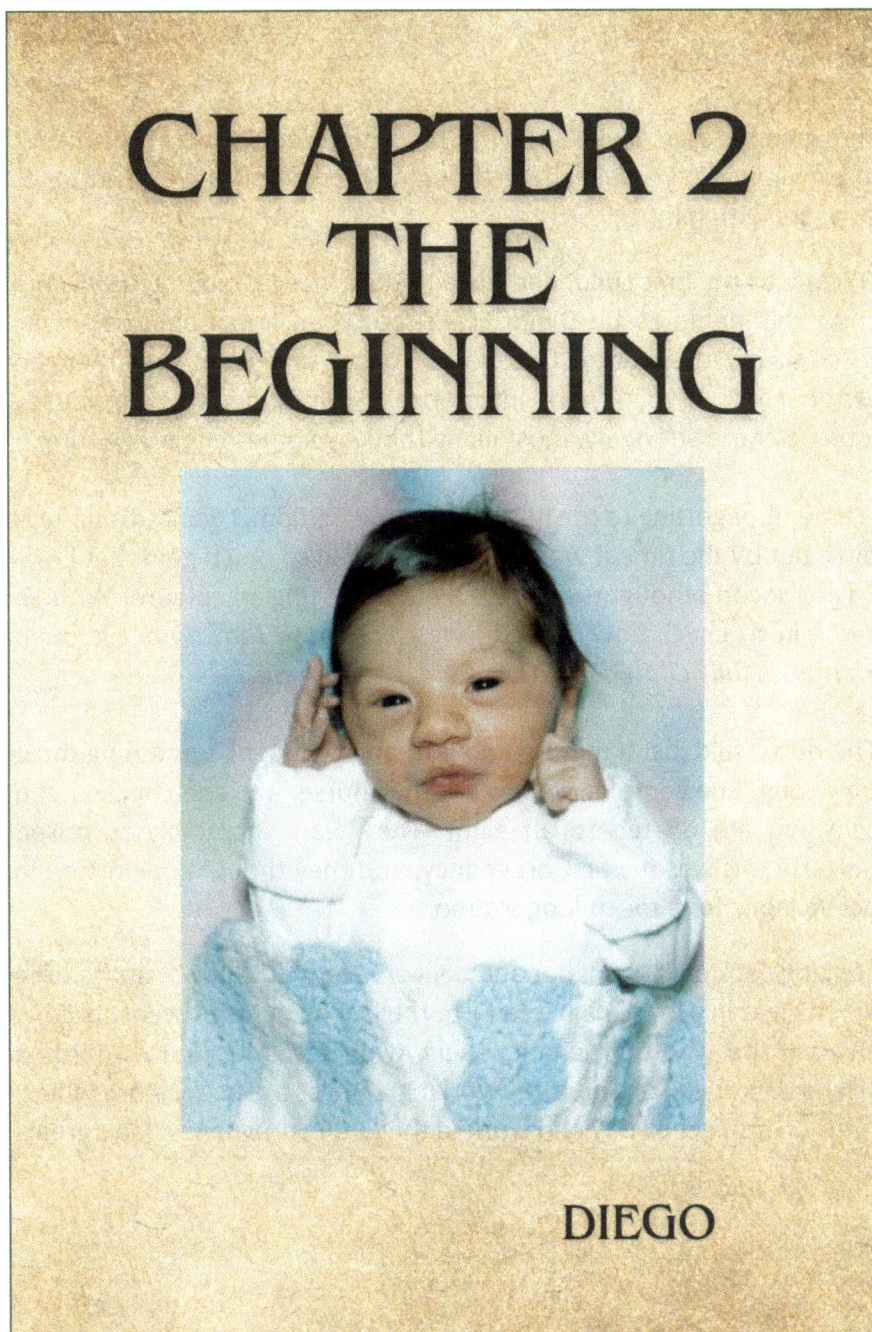

DIEGO

October 4, 1995

I am going to start Diego's story at his birth. When he was born, never in a million years would I have thought I would only have a short 8 or so years with him.

Diego was my first child, and his due date was October 1, 1995. We chose his name to be Diego Fransisco when I was about halfway through my pregnancy. October 1st came and went and then on October 4th, 1995, I went into labor. I remember my dog, Casey looking at me strangely, most likely thinking something was wrong.

I remember getting to the hospital around 6:30pm. I wanted a natural birth but by the time it was 11:30pm I was in so much pain that I was having second thoughts and asked about getting an epidural. A nurse came in to check how dilated I was. *For those that do not know a woman is fully dilated at a ten.*

The nurse said just a minute and left, and I thought something must be wrong. She came back with another nurse, and she checked and said you are dilated to an eight. They were incredibly surprised because this was my first pregnancy, and they thought I would be in active labor for a much longer time.

Looking back on it, my labor and delivery went quickly but at the time when I was in a lot of pain it felt like the last 45 minutes went so slow. Overall, the whole pregnancy went well. I was lucky. No morning sickness to speak of and I was working a job at a grocery store where I was on my feet all day and worked the whole pregnancy. I felt great!

On October 4, 1995, Diego was born at 12:21am. He weighed 6 pounds 6 ½ ounces and 20 ½ inches long. We named him Diego Fransisco.

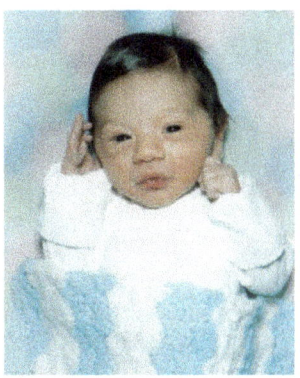

Diego was a very calm baby. He was a happy child and had the cutest dimples when he smiled. He enjoyed playing outside and sports, especially soccer. He loved collecting Yu-Gi-Oh cards.

I remember going to the store with him and he would have his own money and knew he wanted to spend it on Yu-Gi-Oh cards. Diego also excelled in math and was working on his reading and Spanish skills. I remember I had just bought him a workbook so that he could start practicing writing words in Spanish.

When Diego was 5 years & 8 months old, he became a big brother to his sister, Carina. He was so excited to be a big brother and loved to help her. We have many pictures of him holding her and playing with her.

There are so many memories that come to mind when thinking of Diego, however I did not write most of them down, they are just in my mind.

BABY DIEGO

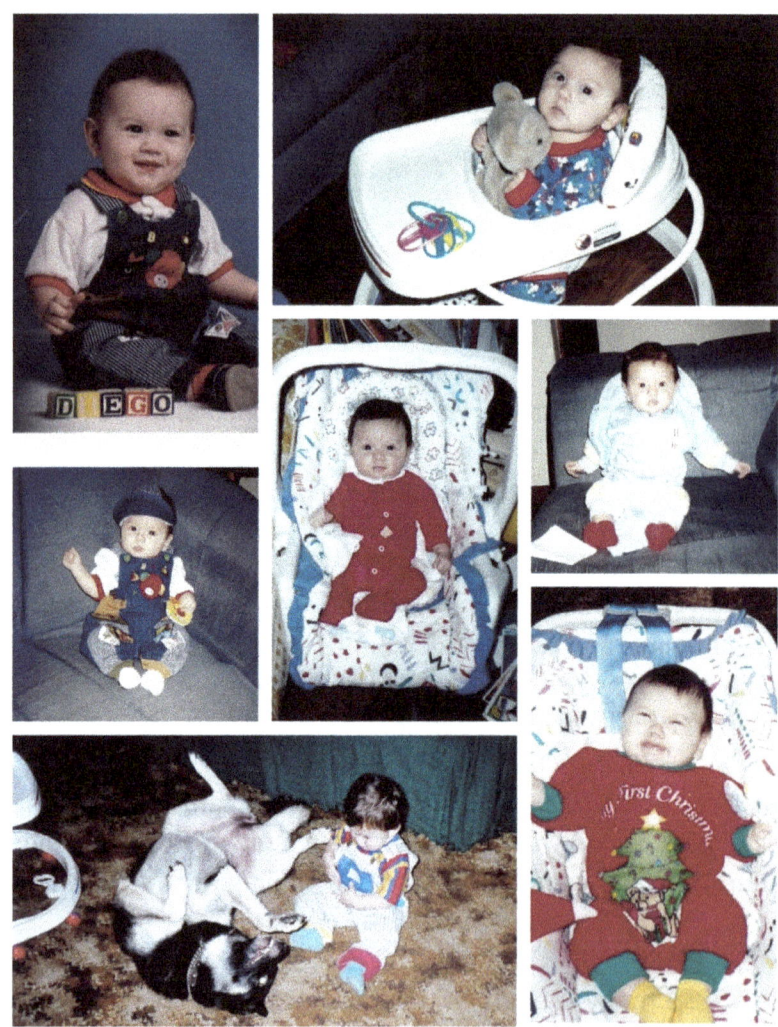

DIEGO

DIEGO

DIEGO AND HIS SISTER, CARINA

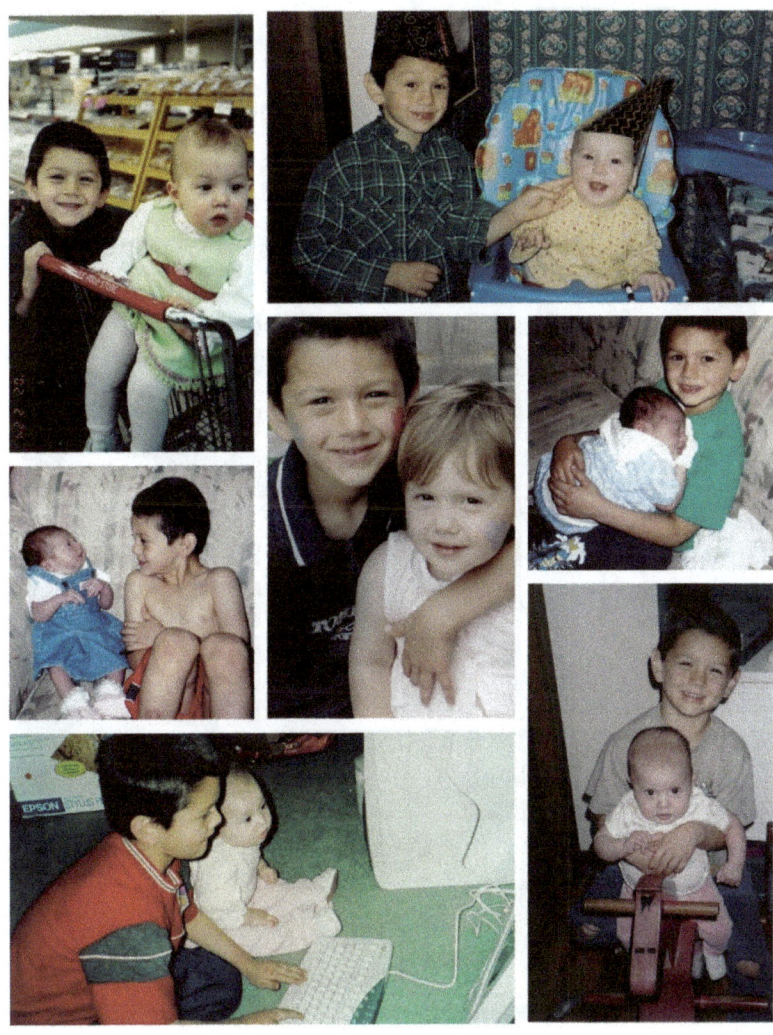

DIEGO AND HIS MOM, KELLY

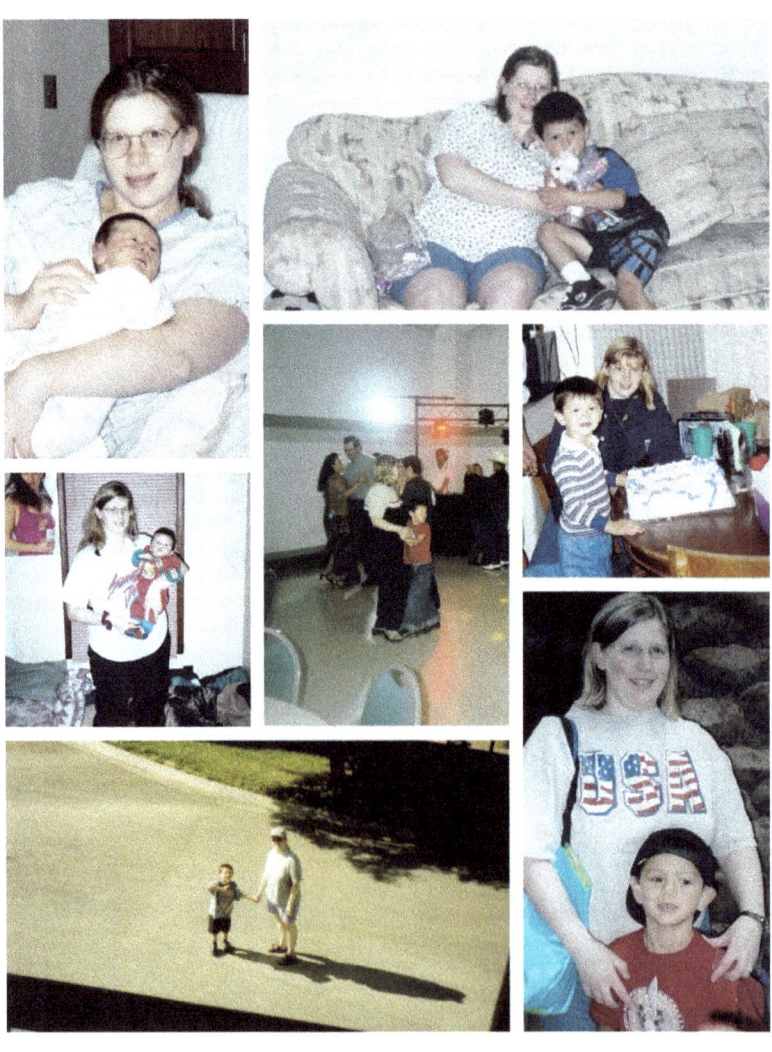

CHAPTER 3
THE WEEK BEFORE

DIEGO

JUNE 19, 2004

Pictures taken on Diego's sister, Carina's birthday exactly one week before his death.

My daughter, Carina, turned three on June 19, 2004. It just happened to be a Saturday, and we had her birthday party that day. It was a fun day with many relatives and friends in attendance at her party.

June 20, 2004 – Father's Day

Diego was going to visit my parents and stay for a few weeks on the farm. He was excited to hang out there with all the animals, my parents, and his uncle, Lance.

This was the last day that I saw Diego.
In 2004 people did not really do video chatting like they do now. So, we talked on the phone a few times that week but what child wants to hang out talking to their mom when there is so much to explore and do outside on the farm.

I remember Diego giving me a massage before he left. He would give me a massage by walking on my back. He was a small-boned child so was not too heavy, so it felt good and did not hurt. The last day that I saw him, he gave me a massage and got his things ready. We were standing on the porch with the sun shining outside. I hugged and kissed him and said, "I love you." He said, "I love you." Then we both said goodbye to each other and then his dad took him to my parents' house.

When I think about this almost 20 years later, it brings tears to my eyes. I was lucky that my last in person interaction with him was positive, that we got to say I love you to each other and goodbye. I have met bereaved parents and others that have lost loved ones, and they did not get to say goodbye or did not have a positive last interaction with their loved one.

I mean, saying goodbye to my son at that moment in time was more like "see you later." I NEVER in a million years thought that it would be the last time I would see him in person and say goodbye. Now years later, it gives me peace to know that I did get to say goodbye to him, in a way.

Diego got a blue guitar and when he went to go to my parents' house he asked if he could take it so grandpa could teach him how to play it. This is one of many memories I have of Diego but since I did not write my memories down, I feel like I lost many of them. I am going by my memory. If you have lost a child, grandchild, sibling, or any other loved one, write down your memories of them, how you are feeling after and other thoughts. Even if you do not want to read them again and never do it is a wonderful way to get your feelings out and the memories down on paper.

Wednesday, June 23rd, 2004
I talked to Diego on the phone briefly. He did not want to talk long because he was having fun on the farm. I do not remember what we all talked about in that brief conversation, but I do remember at the end I said that I missed him, and he said jokingly, "You miss the massages." We both laughed after he said that.

Friday, June 25th, 2004

This is the last day that I talked to my son. My mom called saying that Diego did not feel good. I talked to him and said I could come pick him up and he said, "No, I want to stay here. I just do not feel good right now, but I will feel better." So, I talked to my mom, and she just wanted permission to take him to the doctor if he was still feeling bad later.

He was having a pain in the lower right side of his abdomen. This is the same place where your appendix is. My mom ended up taking him to the doctor and they thought it was just gas since his appendix was already removed 4 months prior. So, they told her to go buy gas drops at the store. My mom was by herself with him and said she was not leaving an 8-year-old in the car by himself. So, she had to bring him inside the store and said he was not feeling good and was weak, so she had to almost be giving him a piggyback ride throughout the store when she went to buy the gas drops.

CHAPTER 4
THE DAY BETWEEN BEFORE & AFTER

DIEGO

June 26, 2004

Have you ever had a day or an experience in your life that now defines the BEFORE and AFTER when thinking of how life was and how it is now? Where NOTHING will EVER be the same again?
June 26, 2004, was that day for me.
I remember that day my daughter, Carina, was with her dad, and I was going to go to a baby shower. I was talking to my boyfriend at the time on the house phone. *I did not have a cell phone at this time in my life.* I was talking to him and should have been off the phone already. *For those of you that do not know me or do not know this about me, I am a time person. What I mean by that is that I am not going to be late somewhere, in fact getting somewhere exactly on time feels late to me.*

We are still talking when I get another phone call beeping in, so I switch lines to answer the other call. It is my dad on the line, and he says to me "Diego doesn't feel good, and we are at the hospital and you, and Francisco *(Diego's dad)* need to get here." We hang up and as soon as I hang up, I am like I should have asked more about how he wasn't feeling good, because my dad said that we both needed to go, and Francisco was with Carina and wouldn't be driving an hour or so just to go get Diego because he wasn't feeling good. It would not make sense for all of us to go to get him.

I called the hospital, *my dad did not have a cell phone either*, because my dad, mom, and Diego were at the hospital. I figure I can call and find out what is going on since I am the mother of Diego. So, I get transferred a few times and end up on the phone with my dad. Which I found a bit odd, then my dad says, "You and Francisco need to get here, Diego quit breathing." Now I do not remember how we all got going but I know that Francisco, my daughter, and I went into my van. Francisco drove and we had to drive just a bit over an hour. That was the longest hour of my life.

On the way, I had a thought pop into my head. The thought was **"He is dead."** Then I had the following thoughts: **"Quit being so negative!" "He is not dead! That happens to other people not to us! Everything will be fine."**

In having these thoughts, my gut/intuition was telling me he was dead. I was hoping my intuition was wrong. We got to the hospital in town. The town that my parents lived in and that I lived in until I graduated high school. It is a small town, with around 8,000 people. Just think of *It's a Wonderful Life* type town. *It's a Wonderful Life is a 1946 film with James Stewart and Donna Reed.*

We walked in and I remember that the hospital personnel were avoiding eye contact. That was not a good sign. We continue walking in and we get to an open door of a room, I see my mom crying and that the pastor of their church is there. I KNEW THEN THAT DIEGO HAD DIED. I remember walking in and the first thing I want of course is to see my son.

They have us sit down and some guy is talking to us. I later found out he was the doctor that tried to save Diego. I don't remember what he all said, but I do remember him talking about grief and in my mind, I am thinking "Quit talking!" I am sure the words in my mind were a bit more explicit and colorful at that moment in time.

We finally got to see Diego. It is Francisco and two relatives of his and I. We decided not to have Carina go in there since she was only 3 years old. When we finally got to see Diego, he probably was dead for about 1 ½ hours, the reason I know this is when I went in there, they had a white sheet covering him and I wanted to see him one last time. I lifted the sheet, and they had already put a tag on his foot! I will never forget seeing that! When I first saw it, looked at the time of death on the tag and it was 3:57pm, and I was glad it was there so I would know what time he died.

We got in the room around 6:00pm. Later, I got thinking about it and thought that it was just awful that I had to see the tag on his foot. It makes me look at movies and shows differently when they show a body with a tag on the toe. My perspective changed on that and on many things in my life. Death just has a way of doing that.
I don't remember how long we were in the room with him, but it felt like eternity, in writing this I am crying now, even almost 20 years later. Yet it felt like I had no time at all to be there with him. After my son's death, time just seemed so different.

We leave the room, and we are all sitting there, and I remember someone coming up and saying that they needed to know what funeral home we were having him go to. I was thinking "what the f***, *I have no idea. I wasn't planning to need a funeral home for my son."* I of course did not say those thoughts aloud. They needed to transport his body to the city to do an autopsy and couldn't do that until they knew where he would be going to after the autopsy. When they asked me if I wanted the local funeral home to recommend one in the town that I live in, I just said yes. I trusted their opinion and even if I didn't, I probably would have said yes still, since I had no knowledge about what funeral home would be good to go to.

Now, we get into a blur of some memories being crystal-clear and some memories not even existing.

Some of my crystal-clear memories:

*I remember my grandmother and aunt coming to my parents' house to see me. It stood out in my mind because my grandmother had two of her adult children die before her so she could understand the feelings of having a child die before us. Which is not in the right order of things. We should die before our children, right?

*I remember calling my boss for my job and telling her and saying I wouldn't be at work tomorrow, because my son died. I remember having a conversation with her and that she was very understanding.

*I remember when I got back home, the next day or so later, I was just leaving my home to go to the funeral home and I saw the back of a boy on a bicycle that looked just like my son, Diego. I have never seen that boy before or ever again.

*I remember being at the funeral home and the director there was saying how strong I was. I didn't feel strong at all but somehow, he thought I was.

*I remember being in the funeral home and this same director was writing up the obituary for Diego and was asking me things that Diego liked. I told him and I know he had to pause for a moment and said these were some of the same things that his son liked. I have seen this director over the years, and he always remembers me and Diego. That gives me a good feeling that we are remembered. I saw him most recently about 4 months ago and he asked how we were doing. He still remembers us.

*I remember when Franciso and I went to the cemetery to pick out the plot where Diego would be buried. They said they could pick one out for us if we didn't want to go. We both decided that we wanted to go and pick out the place where he would be buried. We picked out a cemetery right outside of city limits, it was on a hill and looked beautiful there. Diego died at the age of 8 years – 8 months – 22 days so he could be buried in the baby/children's section. We decided not to do that because it was right by the entrance of the cemetery and right by the road, we liked further into the cemetery more on top of the hill. At the time, in 2004, hardly anyone was buried in that part of the cemetery yet. Now 20 years later, Diego has lots of neighbors!

When we met the cemetery personnel, I remember him saying it is good that you are getting a plot this year. Next year they are going up in price. What??!! I wasn't wanting to get a plot to bury my son EVER in my lifetime. He didn't seem to have any kind of empathy, and it was all business to him. Maybe that is what it needs to be for him to survive mentally working in that field of work. Stood out to me how unsensitive it was to say that to a bereaved parent.

You bereaved know what I mean.

Some of the memories that don't exist for me:

*How did I get to my parents' house from the hospital? I get thinking about this and I have no idea if I drove my van there or what I did. I never asked anyone about this, so I still have no idea to this day.

*I was told that I was on the back porch of my parents' house bawling in the early hours of the morning. I don't remember this at all.

*How did I get back to my hometown that was about an hour or so away? I was told that my sister had driven me home. I don't remember this at all either.

CHAPTER 5
THE DAY SPIDER-MAN 2 WAS RELEASED

DIEGO

Do you remember the day Spider-Man 2 was released?
This is the version of Superman that has Tobey Maguire and Kirsten Dunst. Most of you probably don't remember or have any idea when this movie was released. I mean, why would you? I know if someone asked me when a movie was released, I would have no clue besides that is what Google is for, right?

I can tell you the exact date Spider-Man 2 was released, and I am no trivia expert. It was June 30, 2004. Let me share with you why I know this date but first I will share this: my son, Diego was a big Spider-Man fan! I remember him liking Spider-Man, Teenage Mutant Ninja Turtles, Scooby-Doo, Power Rangers, and Yu-Gi-Oh cards to just name a few of his favorite things. The movie Spider-Man 2 was coming out soon and he wanted to go watch it. I remember he was excited that it was coming to the movie theater soon so we could go watch it.

A random thought: Diego's favorite colors were black and red. Now that I think about it, I wonder if this has anything to do with Spider-Man. This is the first time I have thought about the possible correlation of him loving Spider-Man and his favorite colors. However, I just must guess since he isn't here to ask. How many times have you wanted to ask something or share something with your child or loved one that is no longer with us?

Diego died June 26, 2004. Spider-Man 2 was released 4 days after his death, so we never got to see it together. Not that I was a big Spider-Man fan when Diego was young, but he loved it, and it would have been fun to go with him. So, instead of going to see Spider-Man 2 on June 30th, we were having his funeral that day instead. Diego never got to see Spider-Man 2!

When I initially had this thought, it made me feel sad. Though, I had someone share the thought that Diego was getting front row seats in Heaven and got to see the movie before anybody else. I liked that thought and it brought a smile to my face. What a great reframe of a thought to support me in remembering my son and something he loved.

Years and years went by, and I just couldn't watch ANY Spider-Man movies. I also couldn't watch any Shrek movies for years and years because that is the last movie that Diego and I watched together in the movie theater.

I don't remember exactly how many years later it was until I watched Spider-Man 2 or even Shrek for that matter. I have now watched both many times. I know the first time I watched Spider-Man, I cried and cried. I can feel tears come up as I am talking about it. It was very bittersweet watching the movie alone without Diego. It was sad that I couldn't enjoy the movie with him but now many years later it feels like a way I can connect with my son. In fact, I really like Spider-Man too, it helps me feel close to my son.

==What is something that makes you feel close to your child or loved one that you can enjoy or do in their memory?== This is a fantastic way to keep the connection we have with them. Now many years on or around Diego's death anniversary date, I watch the Spider-Man movie. It supports me in uplifting me and remembering Diego's life, what he liked, etc. on what was the worst time of my life – THE DEATH OF MY SON, DIEGO!

Another memory I have is going to Walmart for the first time after he died. I thought, I could do this. There were so many memories since Diego had gone to the store with me many times. I remember one time when he was debating on whether to buy a bunch of Yu-Gi-Oh cards or to get one big item. I believe on this day he was looking at buying a giant water gun. He would put something in the cart and then change his mind and we would have to go back to the aisle we were in to change back to the other item, which happened a few times until he decided for sure what he wanted. He went for the big water gun that day.

Ok, so going back to going into Walmart the first time after his death, there were tons of memories down almost every aisle. I thought I could go grocery shopping there and be fine, but that day I was not. I had to leave the store. Luckily, I was shopping with someone else at the time and I just got in the car as they finished shopping. I ended up in the car crying and crying. Eventually I could go back to the store and make it through the whole shopping trip without leaving and without any tears.

Now 20 years later, I can shop at Walmart with no issues at all. The intensity changes over time so now if a memory pops up in my mind, I smile and think of Diego.

If you like Spider-Man or end up watching the movie. Just take a moment to think of my son, Diego. I would appreciate it. Anytime you think of my son, it helps me to know he is not forgotten.

Thank you to everyone that came to the visitation and funeral. Thank you to everyone that has been here for me throughout the years!

THE GRIEF JOURNEY WHEN A CHILD DIES

DIEGO'S VISITATION

A Memory about the Funeral Day

The funeral day was the last day I got to see my son's physical body for the last time. We had an open casket at the funeral, and I remember at the end of the funeral all our friends and family walking by to say their last goodbyes to Diego.

In seeing everyone walking by, there was one person that really stood out to me. There was a woman whose daughter was in the same grade and school as Diego. Her daughter went to the same daycare/preschool as Diego did when they were little. I had not ever talked to this woman, and I was curious why she was at Diego's funeral without her daughter. If she was there with her daughter, I wouldn't have had a second thought about it.

Both Diego and this woman's daughter went to the after-school care program at the school. Sometime after Diego's funeral, I went to the after-school program and talked to the staff there and they told me that Becky (the women I saw at the funeral without her daughter) had seen Diego's obituary in the paper. Upon reading it she saw the name of Diego's great-grandmother, Ione. Ione is her aunt. Ione is my grandmother.

WE ARE RELATED! SMALL WORLD!

All through the years we had walked by each other when our children were in the daycare/preschool and in school/afterschool care & we didn't even know we were related!

CHAPTER 6
AFTER...

DIEGO

Diego died on June 26th, 2004. His funeral was on June 30th. Two days later, on July 2nd, his dad became a US citizen. Two days after that it was July 4th, the first holiday without Diego. Then the next school year started without Diego and his sister Carina started preschool. Then October 4, 2004, was the first birthday without Diego here. He would have turned 9 years old. Then came Halloween, Thanksgiving, my birthday, Christmas, New Years, etc.

All these special days/holidays came and went and that first year I was in shock, didn't really feel like it was real, that he was just visiting my parents and would be home soon. For me, in the second year I felt more intense emotions because the first year I was basically in shock and just functioning. By the time it was the third year I felt I was in a place to help others.

It has now been 20 years (when this book was initially published) since he died. Some things seem like yesterday and other things seem like another lifetime ago. Though I will share with you that the intensity of the pain and sorrow isn't as intense as it first was when we had our child or loved one die.
I still have days/times that I miss my son so much and wish he was here, and I have a good old fashion cry at times also. But through the years I have learned to have this "new normal" and still enjoy my life. I still can have happiness in my life and still grieve the death of my son for the rest of my life. It is a journey, a new way of how my life is.

In fact, I had to decide did I want:
- To be unhappy for the rest of my life.
- To cry every day.
- To feel like the victim.
- To feel as if I can't be happy because I had a child die.

I decided NO!

I wanted:
- To feel happiness.
- To have purpose.
- To feel alive.
- To keep my son's memory alive.
- To mention his name. *If someone asks me how many children, I have: I will ALWAYS include him.*
- I want to hear his name and to have others say his name and ask me about him.

In saying this, it didn't happen overnight. If you are reading this and just had a child or a loved one die, know your grief journey is yours and only yours. No two people grieve the same and you have a right to grieve how you would like to grieve, just don't hurt yourself, others, or the environment/property/things.

It is ok to be on this grief journey for the rest of our lives. We just must move through it and feel our emotions so we can be on a healthy grief journey. Not one of destruction. If you feel you are in a place of destruction, depression, etc. please reach out to someone for help, you are not alone on this journey. Reach out to a friend, a support group, therapist, pastor or other professional. If you are in a low place and feeling really depressed and are suicidal, remember you are not the only one that has felt this way and reach out immediately by calling 911 for help. You may also call, or text 988 for the Suicide & Crisis Lifeline for support and resources.

You can also go to 988lifeline.org for information or to chat if you need someone to talk to. You are only in a temporary mindset and there are people out there to help you when you are at your lowest. You are not alone even if you feel you are.

US Citizenship
Going back to the beginning of this chapter, I mentioned that two days after the funeral Diego's dad became a US citizen. Diego's dad and I were not together but I went to his citizenship ceremony as a form of support for his big accomplishment of being a US citizen. I remember sitting by people that were all excited that their loved ones were becoming US citizens.

I felt like I was in some other place. Like everyone around me was in some other world or that I was in some other world, it was a foggy kind of place where I felt I was there next to them but not there. That I could hear everything they were saying but I was looking at my world through a fog of grief and couldn't feel the excitement of the experience. I guess that was the feeling of shock, that nothing was real. That my world wasn't real. I didn't want this new world. The world without my son.

I remember talking to my son not long before he died about his dad becoming a citizen and he was asking me questions about what that meant "his dad being a US citizen." It was a nice conversation where he was curious and excited about it. Who knew that he wouldn't get to be a part of the experience.
I don't know if any of you have had the opportunity to be at a citizenship ceremony. It is a neat experience. I wish I could have been more present in the moment. I took pictures, listened to the speaker at the ceremony, and saw Diego's dad get his certificate and all the new citizens waving their US flags. It was a neat experience. I just wasn't fully there as I would have been since my son had just died 6 days prior.

I remember the speaker talking and he talked about someone that had earned their citizenship but had died before attending the ceremony. He talked about it a bit and it just made me feel like crying and crying. Hearing that this man had died before being able to attend this ceremony made me think just how short life is. That his family never got to see him get his US citizenship just like Diego didn't get to see his dad get his. Though now, 20 years later, I am sure that Diego was watching the whole time from above and got to see his dad accept his certificate of citizenship.

July 4th, 2004
First holiday after Diego's death was Independence Day. I remember Diego enjoying this holiday with all the fireworks, sparklers, and food. This first 4th of July, I just sat in my house as someone else took my 3-year-old daughter to see the fireworks. I just didn't want to be around it all. All of it just annoyed me and I was sad. Especially sad.
I know overall 4th of July was never really my favorite holiday but it was ok especially with having kids and seeing their excitement over the fireworks, etc. But after my son died, it was like I hated the holiday. *And I don't like hating things.* I think that every year that the 4th of July came that it was another year without my son and who wants to celebrate that. I got use to the holiday being one that I disliked and over the years it wasn't as bad, and I even enjoyed it sometimes especially since I had my 3 daughters *(Diego had two sisters born after he died.)* to enjoy it with. But I will still say of all the holidays, I could skip the 4th of July celebrations and not even miss it.

Back to School
It was sad when I saw all the back-to-school things knowing that Diego wasn't here to go back to school. He would have started 3rd grade, and his sister Carina was starting preschool. It was her first year of going to school. It was very bittersweet.

October 4th, 2004
This would have been Diego's 9th birthday. It would have been fun. We would have had food, cake, pinata and friends/family over to celebrate. Instead, we went to the cemetery with balloons and then we had cake. This first birthday, there was myself, my daughter and a few family members that came to "celebrate his birthday" AKA…. remembering him on his birthday.

On this day they still hadn't put up Diego's gravestone at the cemetery. A relative worked for the company that was going to be putting up the gravestone. He called me and let me know what time they would be putting it up in case I wanted to be there. I did. I went there and got to see them put up his gravestone. It was just me and my daughter. It was nice that I could see them do it but of course I wish it were something I never needed to see.

Diego's 9th Birthday was his first birthday in Heaven.

October 18, 2004

This is the date on the autopsy report. I remember it being about 4 months until we got the autopsy report and found out his cause of death. Four months without knowing what caused him to die!

==On his death certificate it says immediate cause of death was: *Septic Shock/Cardiopulmonary Collapse due to Necrotic Bowel & Mesentery.*==

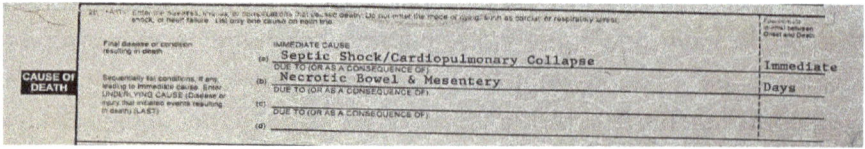

==On the autopsy report it said Probable Cause of Death was: *Septic shock as a consequence of ischemic terminal ileum.*==

I had to look up the words to know what they meant since I had never heard those words before. Why would I have?

Whenever I share with people how my son died, I share that on February 10th only about 4 months before he died, he had surgery to have his appendix removed. On June 26, 2004, he was in the waiting room of the hospital when he went into shock, and they couldn't save him.

What happened is that the way his body healed itself, *where the scar was at the incision site of where they took his appendix out*, blocked the blood to the small intestine and that caused pain and put him into shock. I was told that it is rare to have this happen.

February 2004 - Diego in the hospital after getting his appendix out, little did we know he would gone a short 4 months later.

Halloween

Honestly, I don't even remember what I did on the first Halloween without Diego. I guess I did something since my daughter was 3 years old. But I just don't remember. Maybe someday I will find some pictures I took that day, if I took any that day. Diego loved Halloween. Since his birthday is in October we would always decorate for Halloween, and many times have Halloween stuff around on his birthday too. I think I didn't like Halloween too much at first either.

Maybe that is how all the FIRST holidays were. Though I know through the years I still enjoyed Halloween. It wasn't the same kind of feeling I had towards the 4th of July.

December 18th and 19th, 2004
My birthday is December 18th. It is one week before Christmas and two weeks before the New Year. I am sure my birthday was no fun to celebrate that first year. I don't remember. I probably didn't want to remember.

On December 19th I started not feeling well at all, in fact I thought to myself *"Am I having a heart attack?"* So, I ended up going to the Emergency Room. They did all the tests, etc. and then said something to the effect that during the holidays people get more stressed out so it could be due to stress. I said, *"My 8-year-old son died 6 months ago."* I do not remember exactly what they said but their face expression said it all. OF COURSE THAT COULD CAUSE IT TOO! Oh, and I wasn't having a heart attack, it was just my body's reaction to grief.

Grief. It hurts. It is painful. There are so many feelings to feel. There are ups and downs. And those ups and downs might all be in one day or mixed in many ways during the days, weeks, months, and years.

Christmas 2004
I remember not really wanting to put a Christmas Tree up. We always put a tree up when Diego was alive. It was fun! Lots of fun! Laughter! But Christmas 2004 was no fun! I had my 3 ½ year old daughter so I needed to put a tree up. It wouldn't be fair for her not to have one or to not celebrate Christmas.

I took a different approach. I put my tree up, put lights on it and then bought Angel decorations and only put them on the tree. It felt right to have those Angels on the tree that first Christmas without Diego.

For all of you bereaved parents and others missing a loved one, know you can change your Christmas traditions (or whatever holidays you celebrate). You can make new ones or just do something different one year. Let others know what you need or let them know you might not be making definite plans because you don't know what you will feel like doing that holiday. It is ok. Others might not understand but we really don't want them to ever have to understand, right?

2005
It was time to flip the calendar to the next year, 2005. It felt so wrong to go into a new year without my son here. Most of 2005 I just went through the motions, I am sure. Working, taking care of my daughter, etc.
My second daughter, Jocelyn, was born in 2005 about 10 years after my son was born. So, it is easy to think about how old Diego would be if he were alive. I just took her age and added 10 years.

2007
This is the year my third daughter, Mariana, was born. About 12 years after Diego was born.

2011
I had a miscarriage this year in March. The night before having the miscarriage I had a dream/vision of Diego holding a baby boy. I cried and cried knowing that this baby was with Diego. Crazy, because the next day I found out that I had a miscarriage. I just knew. I was only about 8 weeks along, so I didn't know the sex of the baby yet, but I knew it was a baby boy because I saw Diego holding a baby boy.

October 4th, 2011
This would have been Diego's 16th birthday and 8th birthday in Heaven. I decided to have food and cake at the cemetery and invited friends and family to remember Diego there with me. We took pictures, had balloons and people shared memories of Diego. I got a big birthday cake for Diego, and we took a picture with a bunch of the

kids and the people that were there. I remember a younger kid being confused and asked whose birthday, is it?

We were there for several hours until it got dark out. It was a good time, the only thing missing was Diego. I am sure he was looking down on us smiling as we celebrated his birthday.

2012 - Tattoo
On what would have been Diego's 17th birthday, I got a tattoo in memory of him. I had never gotten a tattoo before and always wanted to get one but was never sure what to get, so I just never got one. They are permanent and I wanted to get something that I would want on my body forever.

I remember going to the tattoo place and asking if I could get a tattoo of my son's first name in his writing. I brought a school paper with how he wrote his name when he was 8 years old. They said yes and asked me about my son. They were so nice and listened to me as I was talking about my son. Talking when getting the tattoo also helped in not feeling the pain as much when getting the tattoo.
Did you ever get a tattoo in memory of a loved one? If you haven't, have you ever wanted to get one?

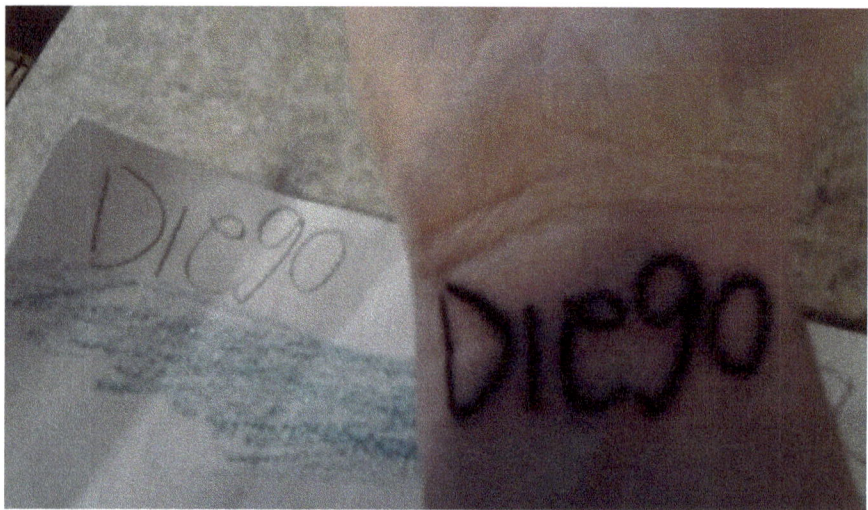

Tattoo that Diego's mom got on what would have been his 17th Birthday.

2014
Diego would have graduated from high school this year. It was also the 10-year anniversary of his death. It is hard to believe that so much time had passed since Diego died.
I thought about going to the High School graduation, but I ended up not going. A part of me wishes I would have gone but when it came to the day of graduation I just couldn't go. I didn't have it in me.

This was also the year that we found out our dog, Max, had cancer and he died. It was a hard year. We used the name that Diego always wanted for a boy dog – MAX. Losing Max felt like losing a connection with my son.

The years kept flying by.
The years went by faster and faster which meant Diego was gone longer than he was here.

2016
This is the year that Diego would have turned 21-years-old. I am not a drinker so I didn't choose to drink on what would have been his 21st birthday but I wanted to do something a 21-year-old would do. So, a good friend of mine took me to the Casino. It was bittersweet. Thank you amiga!

May 2024
My daughter Jocelyn graduated high school this year. How fast the years have gone. Jocelyn is 10 years younger than Diego, and it seems crazy that 10 years had passed since Diego would have graduated high school if he were alive.
It got me thinking of how old he would be now if he were still here. He wouldn't be a little kid anymore, though that is the only way that I picture him in my mind when I think of him. He would have been 29 years old this year. Where have the years gone? Some things that happened seem like yesterday and others seem like eternity ago. I know in my mind he is 29 years old wherever he is, but I still picture him as the 8-year-old I saw the last time on June 20, 2004.

I will always remember my happy, smiling son, Diego, and I feel his spiritual presence by my side. He just isn't here on Earth with me. I know he is watching over me and his sisters as a guardian angel of sorts. I am so thankful that I had the opportunity to be his mom and have him in my life. I just wish it would have been for many more years. I know I can talk to him anytime I want and when I close my eyes, I can see him, and he is responding and talking with me too.

One day, we will see each other again and the reality of it is that time doesn't really exist so in the end it will be as if no time has passed at all. But that will be once I am in the spiritual world, here on Earth time exists so I will enjoy the time I have here on Earth and I know that I will see my son, Diego, again one day.

DIEGO'S SISTERS

CHAPTER 7
RUBY/MAX/MIA

Mia

Max

Ruby

DIEGO

DIEGO & RUBY

In April of 2004, I surprised Diego by getting him a dog. We had a dog named Casey, but she was 12 years old, and I wanted to get Diego a dog that would have his energy level. I remember I went to the animal shelter, and I found a dog that was a mixed breed but looked mostly like a German Shephard and went to pick him up at school. When he got into the van, he had such a surprised look on his face, I wish I had taken a picture. He was so HAPPY!

We went home and had the new dog run around outside and I told Diego he got to name the new dog. I remember the dog running and running outside in the backyard and how happy Diego was. He started thinking of names and I am sure he shared different names which I don't remember all of them since that was like 20 years ago! However, there were 2 names I remember: Mia and Ruby.

He mentioned the name Mia, I think he really liked that name but then said, no he couldn't name the dog Mia because there was a girl in his class named Mia and if he named his dog Mia, she would think that he liked her. Then he mentioned the name Ruby. There was a cartoon on TV called Max and Ruby and that is where he got the name. He said he wanted to get a boy dog and to name him Max. The last 2 months of his life he would mention quite frequently that he wanted to get a boy dog and name him Max.

CARINA WITH RUBY & DIEGO WITH CASEY

April 2004

RUBY AND MAX

I have always been a dog lover. I was raised in the country, and we always had a dog. We had 3 German Shepherds during my 18 years living at home.

1. We had Shadow, a white German Shepherd. She died when I was young.
2. We had Queenie, she was also a German Shepherd. She was what many typically think of when thinking of a German Shepherd. She was black/tan. She also died when I was younger.
3. We had Nikki, also a German Shepherd. We got her when I was 8 years old, and she was still alive when I left home at the age of 18 years old. She was also black/tan in color but a bit lighter color than Queenie. She also had some litters of puppies which was fun to get to be around little puppies.

Once I got on my own, I maybe lived 2-3 years without a dog but then promptly adopted a German Shepherd mix from the animal shelter that was black/whitish in color. We named her Casey. She lived 14 years and 4 months. So lived longer than my son, Diego. In fact, she died two years after him in 2006.

Casey is the dog I had when I got Ruby for Diego. Casey was around 12 years old at that time so was less active hence why I got a 4-month-old dog for Diego.

Ruby and Max – 2011
In April 2011, Ruby died. It was sad because Ruby was Diego's dog and a connection to him. I remember crying and crying when Ruby died and missing Diego even more. This was almost 7 years after Diego's death. At that time, I only had one dog, and it was too quiet in the house without a dog after Ruby died. One month later my mom

said that a dog was abandoned by their home in the country and asked if we wanted him, if he seemed good with the kids.
After Diego died, I had two daughters, his sisters one born in 2005 and one in 2007.

So, we went and met the dog. He was a Cocker Spaniel and a male dog. My first thought was NO. I liked German Shepherd dogs or mixed breed dogs that had German Shepherd in them and female dogs. I had never had a dog that wasn't female and that had German Shephard in them. When I lived at home with my parents, we always had purebred German Shepherd dogs.

When we met him, he was a very calm dog, and the girls really liked him. We found out that he was probably only 3-4 years old, and he was already neutered. Poor dog had cockleburs all in his hair and he probably was starving. We took him home and put him outside and he seemed so content. We had to pick a name for him and guess what name we picked?

MAX of course. I always wondered if Max's name was Max before he got abandoned because he would respond right away anytime we said Max.

In July 2014, we found out that Max had cancer. We did treatment with him to fight the cancer but after only a short 5 months he died. I cried and cried again like I did after Ruby died. This was another connection to Diego since Diego always wanted a boy dog and to name him Max. Another connection was lost.

> **I am sure many of you know this feeling when having secondary losses. The feelings of grief from secondary losses can feel even more intense.**

I decided to think that Diego wanted his boy dog Max so badly that he sent Max to us. And that Max only was with us a short 3 ½ years because Diego wanted his dog as soon as he could. Diego, I hope you are all having a lot of fun in Heaven!

MIA

We got a German Shepherd dog in July of 2016. It was the first time that I got a full-blooded German Shepherd on my own and myself and my girls were so excited. On the drive home we had already named her. I mentioned that Diego liked the name Mia so that is the name we chose. As of October 2024, when writing this, we still have Mia. She is now 8 years old. How the time has flown. Most German Shepherds live to be around 12-14 years old so I know one day when she is no longer here that it will feel like we are losing another connection to Diego.

CHAPTER 8
DREAMS & FEELINGS

DIEGO

Throughout the years I have only had a handful of dreams with my son Diego in them. Here are two of them.

'I had a dream on October 20th, 2004.

In my dream I saw Diego and it seemed very real and I could see him clearly. He told me 'It isn't like you told me it would be.' But I could tell he really liked it there.

I asked him 'What is it like?' and he told me what it was like in a lot of detail. At the time of my dream, I could remember what he told me, and I knew it was things that I quite couldn't understand totally yet.

Then I looked to my right and someone was with me. I believe it was my daughter, Carina, but I couldn't see anything else in the dream clearly except Diego. I went back to look at him and was going to ask him something and he was gone.

When I woke, I had a very peaceful feeling. I also wanted to remember what he told me it was like there, and I couldn't remember. The only thing I remember was about him saying that time doesn't exit like it does on Earth.

I feel that dream gave me some well needed peace.'

Diego's Mom, Kelly

'I had a dream in
September or October of 2005
(In real life I was pregnant and due on November 1st.)

In my dream, I had my baby early and she was born on Diego's birthday of October 4th. Diego came to visit to meet his new sister. I kept thinking he is only here visiting and will only be here for a short time, so I made sure I took many pictures of him. I remember being really happy that he was visiting us.

Then after he left, I looked at all the pictures and he wasn't in any of them. There was a picture of a swing set, and the swing was swinging so I knew he was there, and I thought to myself, 'Oh this makes sense, he is a spirit and that is why his image wasn't showing up in any of the pictures.' I felt calm after this dream also.

Diego's Mom, Kelly

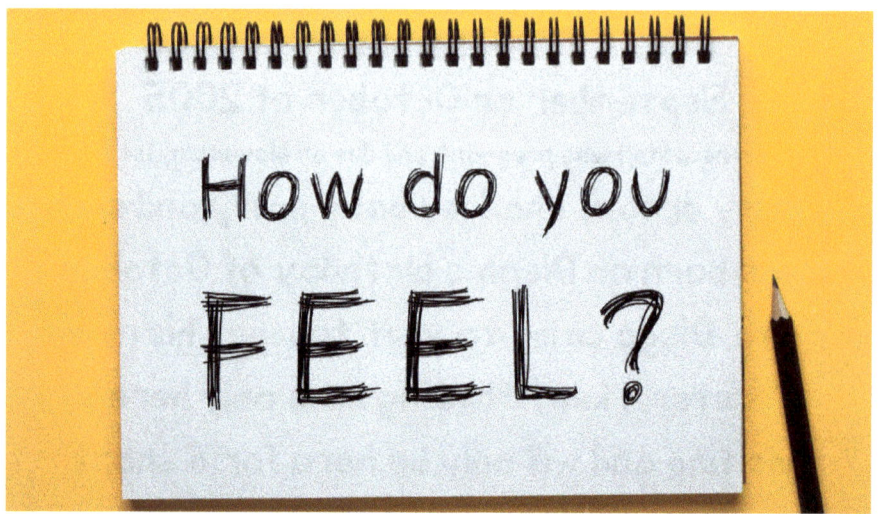

Throughout the grief journey we feel many feelings. I know people sometimes talk about the stages of grief which makes it sound simple, right? It sounds like we just go through the 5-7 stages of grief and get to the other side.

Well, those of us on the grief journey know it isn't that simple. There are so many different feelings to feel during the journey, and you might feel only one per day or all of them in one day.

There are feelings of shock, numbness, sadness, denial, guilt, anger, helplessness, pain, acceptance, and hope, just to name a few.

So how are we supposed to process all these varied emotions and feelings?

Here are some ideas:

- Journal by writing down your feelings, memories, and anything else that will be helpful to write down.

- Talk to a trusted friend, family member, professional such as a therapist or religious leader.

- Go to a support group to share or just to listen.

- Read books about grief and other bereaved parents' stories.

- Do something creative such as making a website, a page in memory of your child/loved one or a memory book (scrapbook).

Do not do unhealthy things that will just make you feel worse later. Remember to not hurt yourself, others or destroy properties/objects.

CHAPTER 9
HELPING OTHERS HELPS ME

DIEGO

For me personally when I help others it helps me.

What do I mean by this?

I mean when I am focused on helping someone else, I am not only focusing on my grief and pain. I am helping someone else, and my focus is on helping them through a hard time or situation.

When my son, Diego died I was fortunate to work in the social service field where I worked alongside nurses, social workers, etc. This is a field of work where you are helping people. When I was working, people including clients, would ask how many children I had, I would always count my son, Diego in the number. At first that number was 2 children, then 3 in 2005 and 4 in 2007. I felt if I left my son out of how many children I have, that it wasn't right. He was still my son even though he wasn't here in the land of the living.

I found in sharing how many children I had and that I had a son that died that many people shared about what they had lost: children, miscarriages, family members, etc. I found in talking about my son, that it gave others permission to talk about their loved ones as well. Talking helps us and others.

A few years after my son died, I started volunteering for The Compassionate Friends. *The Compassionate Friends is a support group for parents, grandparents and adult children of a child that has died of any age and any cause.* I was on the steering committee of a local chapter and facilitated a support group in Spanish for 5 years. Many years later during the 2020 Pandemic, I volunteered by being on the steering committee again and facilitating Zoom video support groups. Weekly at first and then finally back to the once-a-month support groups.

Through the years I have had the opportunity to supported many bereaved parents and individuals. First in the social service non-profit field and now as a coach. *I am a Life and Wellness Coach as well as a Parent Coach.*

I have heard many stories from many people about their children and their grief journeys. In hearing others stories I know I am not alone. That this is a hard journey but none of us are alone. We have different stories, but the main thing is that we have lost a child too soon or a loved one sooner than we wanted to. We may feel alone sometimes but that is common to feel sometimes.

Just remember YOU ARE NOT ALONE!

CHAPTER 10
MARCH 15TH
2008

BRIAN

It is now over 16 years since our son Brian died. Sometimes it feels like yesterday and other times I am amazed that it has been so many years since I last saw him. Brian died when he was 20 years old. It was sudden and totally unexpected. His death was due to a congenital heart defect that he was born with but only detected upon his death.

I started to journal the events surrounding his death at the suggestion of another bereaved mother. I knew that I would never forget what happened that night, however I am glad I took that suggestion to heart. It was difficult to write but it did help me process what happened. There was plenty of crying during the writing sessions, but those painful memories needed to be released.

I began to write one year after his death, and I was already in the process of pushing some of those strong emotions down in a somewhat desperate attempt to feel capable of carving a new path for my life and our forever changed family life.

Brian was a sophomore at the University of Nebraska in Lincoln. He was a student in the fisheries and wildlife program and while at the University, Brian grew into a confident, successful, and academically accomplished young man. He had an amazing girlfriend, many friends and enjoyed sharing an apartment off campus with two fellow students. During his second year, Brian talked about participating in an 11-day ecology study trip with other students and faculty with the College of Agricultural Sciences and Natural Resources Program. The trip would include travel and study in various parts of Puerto Rico. It sounded like an amazing opportunity, and we encouraged him to apply. He came home to visit the weekend before leaving and we were happy to spend some time together. I will never forget that last hug goodbye on our back porch. He was just beaming with excitement! He promised to call us every night to let us know how the trip was progressing. I remember telling him to just enjoy the trip being with friends and colleagues and not to be concerned about us. He could share his adventure once he returned. Looking back on his comments, I am happy that he kept that promise of nightly phone calls.

The group arrived in Puerto Rico and stayed as guests of the University of Puerto Rico on the Rio Piedras Campus. Founded in 1903, this campus is the oldest and largest higher learning institution in the Caribbean. What an amazing opportunity for Brian and his fellow students to experience. As promised, he called to tell us about his first day there. Brian loved to eat, and he shared how he enjoyed the local cuisine and spending some free time on nearby beaches. He toured old San Juan and the Castillo San Felipe del Morro Fort better known as the El Morro Fort.

Our last phone conversation was Friday night. He talked about enjoying a few special drinks. I reminded him to be careful about overindulging in front of his professors. What he said in reply will always amaze me and never be forgotten. He said *"Don't worry about me Mom. I wouldn't want to collapse."* This was somewhat of an unusual remark from him, but the significance of what he chose to say became part of how I was advised of his death. That night Brian talked to both me and John, his father. I got back on the call with him to say goodbye. He told me he loved me and that I should tell his dad that he loved him too. I said I will, and he reminded me not to forget. Brian always ended each phone call that way and I will always be grateful for that. Before we said goodbye, Brian said he would call us again Saturday night. I remember telling him to just enjoy himself and not worry about calling.

That Saturday night, John and I were attending a work-related awards banquet. I checked my phone around 9 PM and saw that I missed his call. I tried to call him back but only got his voice mail. When we got home, our daughter said that she spoke with him and had a great conversation. They talked about his trip for a while and he said that he would call us again around 10:30. That night, I kept checking the phone and kept it close by. I started to think about calling him as I was curious about his day, and I was just plain nosy! I reminded myself that he is a young guy on a trip with friends and should not feel obligated to check in. At times I felt myself getting agitated and worried, feeling a little ridiculous that I was carrying that phone around the house with me as I waited. I finally took the phone to the bedroom and turned it face down on the nightstand. I remember the agitation and worry I was struggling with was replaced with a strong feeling of peace and calmness. I was certain that he was ok. This was around 11 PM, which was 12 midnight in Puerto Rico.

Late Saturday night, the 3rd day of his trip. I got a phone call from the University of Nebraska Dean of Students. Once the Dean was certain that I was Brian's mother, he said *"I'm sorry your son has collapsed and I'm sorry, but he didn't make it."* I remember screaming at John to wake up because someone was telling me that Brian is dead. I did not and could not believe the news that I had just received. I remember feeling shocked, numb, panicked, and a weird sensation of being outside of my own body. While John handled the phone calls, I woke our daughter to tell her about Brian. She later told me that I said that Brian died in a plane crash. She knew this was not possible since she spoke with him a few hours ago. I can only imagine how difficult this evening was for her as she sat with us alone on that horrible first night.

I don't know how John was able to handle all the phone calls, but he contacted the Professor in Puerto Rico and the other family members. I could only sit in shock holding onto Brian's picture.
Our oldest son Mike was able to contact the local police station. We were advised that we would need to travel to Puerto Rico ourselves to identify his body but only via a photo. The police finally agreed to accept a faxed letter from us authorizing the University professor to identify him. This would allow his body to be released to the Institute of Forensic Sciences for his autopsy to be completed.
The next day our home was filled with family and friends, and we were thankful that we were not alone. Later that evening we received a phone call from a reporter based in Puerto Rico. She asked me to tell her about Brian. I don't remember what I told her, but I do remember feeling grateful that she wanted to focus on who Brian was and not how or why he died.

John and I did not know yet why Brian died, but we both thought it was due to a heart related issue. It was the only possible explanation that made sense to us. Two days later, we received word from Puerto Rico, that his autopsy, revealed his heart was missing a major artery which we did not understand. It was only after we received a copy of his autopsy report that we were able to comprehend that one of his major arteries was defective. His heart was not receiving enough blood and oxygen and as he grew older, his heart became enlarged, scarred, and weak. If he had survived his cardiac arrest, we were told that he would need an immediate heart transplant.

We continued to learn more about the events of that evening the next day. Brian along with 3 friends were returning to the University of Puerto Rico dorms after spending some time walking around the nearby university area. He became tired and out of breath. He passed out, fell forward onto the sidewalk, and split his chin open. His friends called for help, provided CPR, and ran to alert their professor. An ambulance was called for, but the requested medical care did not arrive very quickly. Brian died on the street corner with his friends that stayed with him. They will always hold a special place of love and gratitude in our hearts.

Once the ambulance arrived, he was taken to the neighborhood hospital. We later learned that they administered multiple rounds of care to revive him but ultimately, we know he died instantly and quickly. This is the only way I can think of his death and feel some small amount of comfort. Months later, we had a cardiologist review his autopsy report and he confirmed his death was swift and that Brian felt no pain. Maybe that wasn't completely the case but that is what we chose to believe.

One year later, we traveled to Puerto Rico with the sole purpose of experiencing what Brian did on this trip. I was adamant that I needed to see where he died. We met with the Dean of Students from the

University, and we were treated with an abundance of compassion and kindness. She took us to where he stayed at the dorms, the street corner where he died and to the small local hospital. We were able to obtain a copy of his medical records which provided us with more details about his death and multiple attempts to revive him.

HIs medical records indicated his time of death was around 11 PM. When I was feeling agitated and upset waiting for his phone call, that was exactly when he had collapsed. Remember he told me on that last phone call that he did not want to "collapse" in front of his companions and the Dean chose the same words. He died when I finally put the phone down and felt peaceful and calm.

Some things about his death and the choice of words expressed that night remain remarkable and not easy to explain. It is hard for me to provide the explanation, but I believe that Brian was saying goodbye to me and letting me know that he was ok. It will never matter to me what other people may think. I know this was exactly what happened and what I experienced as his mother. Brian and I were close, and he was saying goodbye.

Brian was finally home the following Thursday evening, which was Holy Thursday. I remember begging the funeral home to let us see him that night, but they denied that request and we had to wait until the following day. Seeing his body in that casket was undeniably the worst moment of my life yet I remember feeling immensely grateful that he was home. I thought about how beautiful and peaceful he looked. Under all the sadness and despair, I also felt the most powerful amazing unwavering love for him.

John and I started to attend meetings of The Compassionate Friends Support Group several months later. This is an international support group for bereaved parents, grandparents, and siblings. Here we met with other bereaved parents who bravely shared their stories of loss. We felt connected with others who could understand our despair, confusion, and sorrow. There was no need to explain our feelings and emotions because here with other parents we felt understood and supported. As we listened to those stories, I could feel their pain and anguish, but I also could acknowledge the possibility of surviving the loss. At these meetings, we learned the value of telling the "death story." As we grieve and mourn the physical loss, telling the death story repeatedly helps us to process what happened. We struggle to understand and seek answers to so many questions. But each answer received brings forth only more questions. The cycle of questioning, seeking understanding and finding some level of acceptance only adds to the painful process of where we will eventually need to go, which is to acknowledge the loss and begin the work of rebuilding our lives. This rebuilding takes time and enormous amounts of emotional work. It is not easy.

At one meeting, another parent further out on her grief journey explained that as time goes on, we begin to think less about our child's death, and our thoughts and conversations become more about their life and love. This is a huge corner to turn, and it was a corner I did not anticipate experiencing but slowly and eventually I did. Every little "corner I turned" was a small step towards the goal of putting the shattered pieces of my life and heart back in place. But we soon learned that many of those pieces will never fit again. The dreams I had for my future with my son, the anticipated significant milestones he talked about, those dreams would need my courage and self-compassion to let them go.

I will always continue to share my story with the hope that other bereaved parents can feel supported and understood. Hearing other parents speak of their indescribable loss weighed heavily on our already shattered hearts but we were filled with compassion and the powerful knowledge that we were not alone. We felt especially close to other parents who like us, experienced the death of their child as a young adult.

Regardless of the age of death, there is no denying that the loss is difficult, but the death of a young adult child is a unique kind of heartache. We put in all those hours, days, months, and years caring for them, worrying about them and delighting in their achievements and accomplishments. We journey with them as they reach each anticipated typical milestone. Their first step and first word, the first tooth gone! We delight in their toddler and preschool years when we can talk for hours about their overall cuteness and the funny silly things they say and do! We treasure that warm fuzzy feeling we have looking at their tiny painted handprints on a simple Mother's Day card. Soon we are participating in their Kindergarten round-up and we find ourselves entering another phase of their life. The elementary school years seem to fly by so quickly, and we are present at every game, concert, and parent-teacher conference.

Maybe we will find ourselves working extra hours making tough financial decisions to afford after-school activities, camps, and hobbies. During their time in high school, we stay up late waiting for them to come home safely and silently groan a bit as their curfew gets extended as they get older. We see their excitement and nervousness about their first date. We may be feeling apprehensive while they are feeling eagerness and exhilaration when they get behind the wheel of a car! We are with them as they navigate the decisions and choices for their life after high school. We tag along on college trips and have endless discussions about college funding and their living arrangements away from home. Once Brian started his college years, I trusted that the focus of our time as parents would change as he stepped into the next chapter of his life. We were still mother and son, but we were able to enjoy time together as adults in a redesigned relationship, that unique relationship that includes being friends as well.

I love the memory of Brian graduating from High School. He approached me asking about his curfew. Can he stay out later? I remember feeling a mixed sense of relief and pride as I told him that he was now old enough to decide that for himself. My advice was to stay safe and be smart. That really made him quite happy! I was proud of who he was, and I was relieved that I could finally go to bed and fall asleep without waiting for him to come home. After all that we contributed to their lives, the time, the worry, the financial adjustments, the shared family moments, their death, especially when sudden, feels like that future relationship has been cruelly torn away from us. My relationship with Brian was just simply the best when he died. There are no words to truly explain the depth and pain of this loss, and I could not foresee a future where I would be happy again knowing that his life ended and mine would continue without his physical presence.

But over the years, I did find ways to fill that empty space in my heart and in my life. I was able to see that life can be "good" again and that we can feel grateful that we had the opportunity to experience the depth and beauty of the love we had for our child. I want other parents to know that even after months, years and decades pass, we will still courageously miss our child every day.

Love never dies and our relationship with our child can continue to flourish and be real. It will never be the same way and the way we so desperately want. But we can choose to fill the empty space in our hearts with as much beauty and love as we can find. It takes hard work and time. There is no set amount of time to reach a place of peace. This journey is as individual to us as our child was. We can find ourselves overwhelmed with advice and suggestions on how to grieve and mourn our child. We may find some suggestions helpful, and we may hear others that are hurtful. I came to realize that people will say things that are meant to be comforting but sometimes their advice or comments can be upsetting. I often found myself confused about my grief process and at times almost ashamed that I was not showing the progress that other people thought I should be making. I wondered what was wrong with me!

Here is what helped me the most: I realized that I was the only mother Brian had, and I knew my son in a way that no one else did. Our bond was unique to us. I was the only one that could truly know how to grieve for him. This was a powerful moment for me as I realized that I was doing ok, but I was not always doing fine. I was doing the best that I could, and I accepted that I would have rough days for a long time. But I knew I was going to make it through just like so many other mothers living with the same loss.

We may find comfort leaning on a trusted team of support, but we need to oversee how that team supports us and who we can trust to be part of that circle. I came to recognize that the world is full of compassionate supportive people. Those are the people I kept close by. I created and leaned on my own "Team Brian:" I also experienced situations where I had to accept that for whatever reason some people could not be supportive in a way that is helpful to me. We are not always easy to be around. We are hurt, scared and overwhelmingly sad. We may find it impossible to control the crying. We may be angry and want to be alone. We are struggling to understand how our lives can continue without the physical presence of our child.

We need time and the amount of time it takes is different for all of us. I think one of the most challenging things about being around a bereaved parent is acknowledging the possibility that something like this could also happen to them. And so, it can be uncomfortable and unsettling being in our company. We can care best for ourselves when we acknowledge that we need to let some people stay outside of our immediate grief support circle. We can choose to limit our time and interactions with less supportive people. We can still love them but keep our distance for a time as we prioritize caring for ourselves. The people who can walk with us, sit with us during our darkest times and just be with us through the full array of our emotions and sorrow are out there. Those are the friends and family that will be the best to keep in our own unique grief team of support.

CHAPTER 11
COURAGE

BRIAN

Fear was not an emotion or state of mind that I would have associated with deep grief, but that quickly changed when my son died the Saturday night before Easter weekend in March 2008. While we waited for his body to return to Omaha, we knew we had to decide on how we would acknowledge our final goodbyes. On that Holy Thursday morning, I found myself sitting alone in a darkened church. I had no idea what to do there as I had not attended services for some time. I had asked a friend to please pick the hymns for the service. I could not complete this task. How do mothers "pick" songs or readings for their child's funeral? We pick their food, clothes, and their toys. We chose their first school and values we wish to see them emulate. Before long we see that they are old enough to make their own choices. We learn to step aside and hope we pick the right time and best way to offer any advice or suggestions or just decide to remain quiet and trust they will choose their path wisely.

That morning, I opened the biggest hymn book I could find, not bothering to review the suggested songs for funerals. I found "On Eagles Wings" which is a song I love, and Brian loved birds of prey. I found two additional songs with messages that I believed spoke to his character. As I sat there crying alone in the pew, I felt this small yet powerful surge of courage. I knew that I could do this for him and for our family. I felt an inner strength that filled me with a sense of purpose. Over the next few days while working together as his parents, John and I managed to choose the hymns and the readings for our son's service.

The courage I felt then certainly did not stick around as we grieved for our son and waited for his return home. Any courage I felt was weak and often crushed by the deep sorrow, sadness, and the massive amount of fear that I experienced. My fear was intense and frightening. I feared the truth that Brian had died, and we had no chance to say goodbye. I feared his safe return to Omaha. I feared phone calls in the middle of the night, and I was afraid of losing John, Brian's father and my daughter, Molly. I feared for our other children, grandchildren and those we loved. I now knew how life can change in an instance. I feared facing another day without Brian and I feared the nights where I had to accept that Brian was truly gone. I feared facing the moment when the lid would close on that box. I feared the future, and I feared I would lose my mind. The death of my mother 2 months after Brian died just provided encouragement for my fear and anxiety to intensify.

That intense fear and anxiety did finally soften, and my courage and strength slowly grew stronger each passing day. But when I think back to that day in church doing the unthinkable task of planning Brian's funeral, I can't help but wonder if this was truly an act of courage. After all, I was just being a mom, Brian's Mom. I was doing something for him and because of him just like I did all those years he was still with us. I wasn't going to stop being Brian's Mom but that role as his mother had certainly changed.

Brian and I had many wonderful conversations about life, but we never spoke about dying and how we would want to handle our goodbyes. Before his body was released from Puerto Rico, we were advised that they wished to cremate him. I could not imagine having only his ashes returned to us. I knew that I had to see him to know and believe that it was really my son. We worked with a local funeral home to have his body flown home and to begin making some extremely tough decisions. It was an agonizing 5 days of waiting for that homecoming to happen. Having the traditional funeral home visitation and a catholic funeral was the only option we considered. Brian received all the traditional sacraments in the catholic faith. He was not actively practicing but I felt that a catholic funeral service was the best choice that we as his parents would make for him. I never really considered any other option to think about or decide upon.

We could not bury Brian the weekend he came home as it was Easter weekend. We had to wait until the following week. So, we prepared the only way we knew how. The entire immediate family gathered at our house to make posters displaying his pictures and highlighting his awards and achievements. This display was a chance to show those in attendance who Brian was and for what he will be remembered. It was our way of celebrating his life. We shared this display at both the mortuary and the church.

I remember very little about the actual funeral. Saying that last goodbye before the service began was pure torture. I remember giving him a final kiss goodbye on his cheek, touching his hands and arms, looking at his beautiful handsome face for the last time.

I also remember hearing a comment from someone in the gathered crowd. *"Brian would not have liked this."* I remember hearing those words but not reacting to them. I was too numb and distraught to respond. But days afterwards, I revisited that comment and felt sad, agitated, and hurt. There were a lot of thoughts, love, anguish, and hard decisions made regarding how we chose to say goodbye. We did not have the privilege of knowing what Brian would have wanted. Brian's father and I had several conversations about the funeral service we planned. We both thought that maybe Brian would have told us to cremate him and spread his ashes into a lake, in a forest or maybe at the top of a mountain. He loved the outdoors and was a true nature lover. We wondered if he would have told us to donate his body to science and donate as many organs as possible. But we did not have those conversations, so we chose what resonated with us at that difficult time. It took a massive amount of courage to prepare and plan his burial.

Regardless of how we choose to say our goodbyes and bury our loved one, the funeral service whether traditional or more modern, whether it is in a church, a home or any other gathering place, its purpose is to bring family members and friends together for support. It is primarily for those who are left behind. I am proud of the beautiful and meaningful service we had for Brian. If I could talk to him today about it, perhaps he would have said it would not be his choice but knowing Brian, he would have told me. *"Mom, you do what you and Dad think is best and know that I am with you and support you every step of the way."* Maybe I overreacted to the comment, but that is something that can happen when our grief is so overwhelming. Some remarks can be comforting, and some can be seen or felt as hurtful. We are not thinking, feeling, or acting with calmness or clarity. We are in shock, scared and broken.

The entire first year after Brian died was difficult, full of turmoil, despair, sadness, anger, hopelessness and that same feeling of fear and dread. I couldn't sleep, eat, concentrate on work or other responsibilities. I could not control the playbacks of the words spoken to me on that phone call. I was exhausted physically and emotionally. I had my first panic attack while at a favorite store where Brian and I had enjoyed several shopping trips. I remember feeling overwhelmed with the knowledge that Brian was truly gone. The fear became so suffocating that I had trouble breathing and felt my heart pounding and racing. I had to immediately leave the store.

I had those same panic attacks when visiting his grave. I wanted to go to the cemetery with John, but the severe anxiety symptoms made the visits impossible for me. Knowing he was buried underneath where I stood was agonizing. Every Sunday we would go out to the cemetery and each week I could get a little closer before I had to turn around and leave. On one visit as I got closer to his grave, I felt comforted with the realization that Brian and who he was as our son were not there, it was only his body. I could and would feel his presence in other more meaningful places and times. After that I was able to stand together with John at the grave to remember the love we had for our son. It was still never easy, but I was able to be present without panicking. Going to his grave was something that we could still do for him together as his parents.

A few weeks after the funeral, I contacted my doctor and requested medication for the anxiety and sleepiness nights. Taking that medication was the right choice for me. I was able to control the panic attacks and sleep well. I was still grieving and crying but getting to sleep allowed me to have moments where I could rest without the overwhelming fear and anxiety. I never worried that I would become totally reliant on the medication, I just felt confident that I would use it only when truly needed. After a few months, I was able to try sleeping without the medicine and found that I was able to gradually leave it behind. Intense grief can weaken the immune system and leave us feeling depleted and vulnerable to a variety of physical ailments and illnesses. Although restful sleep may seem like an impossible reality, we need the rest to combat the physical stress of our grief. We can try mediation, journaling, relying on our faith and finding support with others. I tried many coping tools, but I felt that I needed additional help. We just must do the painful work of discovering what tools would work for us, knowing that every tool we use may be different at different parts of our journey.

I never imagined I would survive that first horrible year of missing him. But on the 10-year anniversary of his death, I was able to look back and see the progress I made. I could recognize that I was in a different place, and grateful that I had not settled into a place of bitterness and constant sorrow. I struggled in those early years as I felt angry that this happened to our family and that Brian lost out on so many opportunities to live a longer life.

So, what really got me out of that deep dark hole? My practice of gratitude. Gratitude for his life, his accomplishments, and for the joy and experience of being his parent. I focused on as many memories as I could and would often just close my eyes and try to remember the funny things he would say, the intensity he showed playing his drums, his love for Lacrosse and that last hug. I remember our conversations about what he wanted to accomplish in his future. He had big plans, and I loved that he shared his ideas with me. I used those memories to lift me up and provide substantial fuel for my soul.

Memories brought forth smiles, laughter, and reminders of how life's priorities are forever changed and are seen in a different light.

I focused on gratitude for John who is the only other person on earth that knows what it was like to be a parent to Brian. I was grateful for our other children, their spouses, friends, and family. I was grateful for my belief, although a somewhat quavering belief at times, that Brian is in heaven, and I will know him again someday. I am not saying that I understand all that this involves but I used this belief to fuel my determination to live my life fully and gratefully.

It is now over 16 years for my grief journey, and I am strong enough, confident enough to suggest to other bereaved parents that one way out of the despair is to explore your own way of seeking hope. That powerful place of hope is as individualized to each of us as our relationship with our child was. Life can go on; it just goes on differently and certainly not as planned. It takes hard painful work which in the beginning can be at times debilitating work. It hurts and we feel that pain physically as well. After Brian died, I know I was living in a very deep and dark place. Climbing out of that hole was incredibly hard. I would experience times of hope and gratitude but then slide back down again to days filled with sadness and hopelessness as I longed to see him again, hear his laugh and enjoy another one of his strong hugs. It was a long tough fight to continue moving forward as that way forward and up was indeed a very slippery slope to navigate.

It was only after many years that I was able to look back and see how far I traveled away from that consuming place of sadness. Yet I never want to forget that place of despair because I know that the depth of my sorrow was so beautifully woven and interconnected to my love for Brian. It is hard work to gather renewed strength, courage, and fortitude to anticipate a revised future without the physical presence of our child. It takes immense courage to continue going forward and learn to focus on the goodness and beauty we still have within our reach. We will always have our child and their love with us, and that love will never be lost or forgotten. We can choose to maintain that connection with them, and we can have the strength and courage to build on that connection in our own way *taking all the time we need.* We can have our life continue to be full of goodness and beauty. Time does not heal all our wounds, but the passage of time can soften the pain and sorrow.

> **We may never return to who we were before the loss. We will be different people rebuilding our lives while we remember The Love.**

JOANN & HER SON BRIAN

CHAPTER 12
MOVING FROM GRIEF TO GRATITUDE WITH PILATES

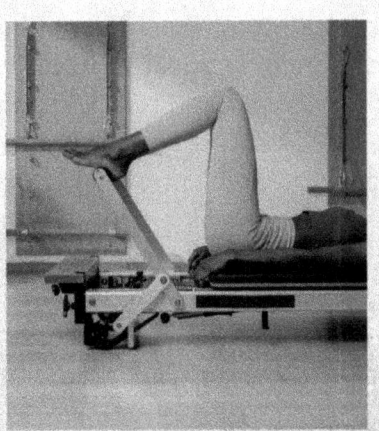

BRIAN

The death of a child affects parents physically, emotionally, spiritually, and cognitively. It is one of the worst traumatizing experiences any parent can face. This extreme grief is hard, demanding, physically draining, and just exhausting. It is not unusual for newly bereaved parents to experience flashbacks while learning how to cope with the loss. We can be catapulted back to that moment in an instant. The moment we answered the phone call or responded to the knock on the door. That was the moment we were literally brought to our knees. We can find ourselves reliving that moment repeatedly during those initial days, weeks, and maybe even months.

Brian's father and I learned that creating our own personal grief toolbox was the best way to cope with and manage this huge change in our life. One of my tools was Pilates. My Pilates practice helped me strive towards becoming grounded again. The breath pattern calmed down the constant emotional chaos and softened the anxiety. The exercises required both mental and physical concentration, which helped me stay grounded in the present moment. The verbal cues that I came to treasure provided a way to engage my mind with other images and provided a respite from reliving the moment I learned of Brian's death. The movements were soothing and comforting. Feeling my body move, my muscles contract and stretch was life affirming for me. Pilates encouraged me to experience hope, and hope is what I desperately needed to find.

Practicing Pilates also helped me to gradually move away from the more physically demanding exercise I was doing. I rode my bike over 100 miles a week. I walked, jogged, and ran miles trying to push away the intense emotions and pain. Pilates helped me acknowledge that no amount of pounding my body into the ground for days, weeks and months will completely take away my pain. You see, it is not just sadness and despair we feel when our child dies, there can also be anger, bitterness, regrets, and guilt. The "why" "how" and "if only I had" scenarios we envision can truly wreak havoc on our ability to function so that we can "re-enter" back into our work and/or family responsibilities.

My son's death was indeed the catalyst for my decision to pursue additional Pilates training. Brian was an athlete throughout his high school years and lacrosse was his favorite sport. He valued exercise and movement as much as I did. On the last weekend before he died, we spent time sharing our favorite exercises. To this day it is one of my fondest memories of time spent together. After his death, a friend told me that Brian was impressed with my Pilates practice. I decided immediately that studying and teaching Pilates was going to be my way of honoring his memory and maintaining a connection with him. But for me to pursue additional training, I had to move past my negative self-image. I did not believe that I was capable of diving into a more advanced training program. I always struggled in school and lived most of my adult life with low self-esteem and confidence.

Two years after his death, I woke up one morning with this amazing epiphany. I was surviving a horrible life altering situation. I began to believe in myself in an entirely different way. I knew that since the worst possible thing had already happened to me and I am surviving my son's death, I can surely find the courage to try and achieve this dream. If my attempt is not successful, it will be okay. It will never be the worst thing in my life to live with. I found the courage to take that training, received my advanced certification, and have cherished teaching in my son's memory for over 12 years. Through my teaching I can share how important it is to move our bodies, to strengthen and stretch our muscles. We can honor our bodies as they are and to be grateful for the opportunities a more conditioned body can lead us to. We may never know why Brian's heart stopped beating when it did, but his doctor said that he likely lived a longer life despite his heart condition because he did exercise. What an amazing powerful message for all of us!

We have no choice regarding our child's death, but we can choose how we treat and care for ourselves during this stressful journey, because this journey will never end but only change and evolve. As bereaved parents, we experience the inability to protect our child. Even if we know rationally that we could not have prevented their death, emotionally we can be left with a deep wound. Parents are supposed to protect their children, yes, we may even feel that responsibility when our children are adults. That is one of our main parenting roles. We may know intellectually that their death was not our fault, but finding peace in our hearts can be a monumental undertaking.

I love to watch ABC's Good Morning America, and I especially appreciate Robin Roberts, the anchor of the show. She was diagnosed with and survived a difficult health challenge. She learned from her mother early on to "make your mess your message." One morning I listened to her explain that regardless of what tough situation you are facing, we can strive to understand it. Robin suggests you can determine if there is a way that you can share what you learn with others to help them on their journey. Then I heard her speak of her health situation and how she relied on her mantra, I added her words to my grief toolbox. Because of my son's death, Pilates became my passion and my message. I found that I could ease some of my grief by sharing this passion with others and encouraging others to value exercise as another tool to rely on when our stress level is rising to an unhealthy level. Our challenging life experience can involve the death of a child, a serious illness, financial struggles, or broken family relationships but the message I love is encouraging others to take action to manage life challenges and any resulting emotional pain. Choose what method of movement resonates with you personally and strive to include some movement in your life when you can.

Making "my mess" my message did help me feel connected with Brian. It provided me with hope that I can rebuild a good although very different life. I can find a new purpose in my life and this new redesigned purpose can slowly help me to acknowledge and accept that my anticipated future was forever dramatically altered. I can once again feel grateful for my life and for the time that we had with our son.

CHAPTER 13
MY FAITH JOURNEY

BRIAN

My Faith Journey and Where Do I Go from Here?

I must admit that before Brian died, I was on the fence regarding my faith and what I believed about life after death. Both our son and daughter attended a Catholic elementary school, and I prioritized attending the mandatory weekly school mass with them. My attendance at Sunday service was sporadic. Since I was divorced and remarried outside of the Catholic Church at times, I felt uncomfortable, unwelcome, and confused about my "status."

Over the years, I decided that if the God spoken about in church was loving, forgiving and supportive, then I would leave the ambivalence behind. I would believe in a supreme presence who first and foremost would be happy that I was taking the time to be part of a community of believers. I believed in a God who did not see me as unworthy or unwelcomed, but I trusted that my life, my values, and my actions were the most important aspect of my spiritual and earthly journey.

Before Brian died, my prayers were simple and direct. Please keep my children safe, healthy, and free of any physical or emotional pain. I believed that this was the best way to pray for them. Reflecting on this, it seems I was directly asking for the biggest favor and special considerations from the ultimate superior being! If I were following the commandments, practicing kindness, doing volunteer work, being a good parent, supportive wife, my prayers would be heard, and my requests would all be granted. I believed in Heaven and that I would be judged at the time of my death whether I personally would be granted access to this wonderful place of eternal life. Basically, I didn't give much thought to the existence of Heaven, I just accepted this as fact. At times, I did have doubts about the existence of life after death, but I never spent the time or energy to believe without any doubt or questioning.

Several years before Brian died, I attended a church program for people seeking a return to the Catholic Church. During one conversation with another participant, I was referred to as a "cafeteria catholic." She explained that I was only picking and choosing what I wanted to believe in, and I am not following all the catholic religion's beliefs, practices, and teachings. I decided that I am good with that description! I choose what to believe in based on my own free will and common sense. I think this is what God would want us to do. Decide for ourselves. Be a good person, be kind and respectful to those we meet and those we hold dear to our hearts. Cherish your time here on earth and cherish our physical world and all its beauty. I do go to church when I feel I need the connection. I don't worry about what day it is, I focus only on why I need to be there. I want comfort, connection, and hope.

After Brian died. I was incredibly angry at the God who I thought would and should be protecting my son, my daughter and all my family. I was quite sure that I had requested their safety the best way I was taught during my years receiving a Catholic education. At times I thought I was perhaps being punished for past sins and life choices. If I wasn't going to blame myself, I had to blame someone. I directed my fury and hostility to the supreme being who I believed rejected both me, my family, and my daily prayers. I would hear the comments from some people that Brian's death was all part of God's plan. They told me that God has his reasons for allowing this tragedy to happen and maybe God just needed another angel in Heaven! I would only reply that there were plenty of talented souls already there, so my son was truly not needed.

I hated to hear the comment that "Brian is in a better place." The best place for Brian was to be here on Earth, living a much longer life with those of us who knew him and loved him. I realized that people offered remarks they believed would be comforting but at times those remarks caused me more anguish and confusion.

But I desperately needed to believe that Brian was "somewhere." I needed to believe in a future where I would see him and know him again someday. I slowly began to accept that my anger towards God would not be healthy for me. I started to spend one hour each week in the church chapel. I chose this place because it was the last place I had the gift of seeing my son. I spent the hour reading about grief, faith, and hope. It was emotionally draining but here I felt comforted and close to Brian.

During that first year, I heard about a Presbyterian church that held a service where dogs were welcome to attend with their owners. Although I did not have my own dog at the time, I was curious enough to attend. When I met the pastor at the door, she asked me where my dog was. I explained that our last dog died the day after our son's funeral. Without a single moment of hesitation, I asked her, *"Why did God take my son?"* She replied with what I thought was the absolute best answer. She explained that God did not take my son, but he was there to welcome him into Heaven. I thought now that is something I can live with. This can bring me peace and comfort. Brian was welcomed and loved. He was not left behind someplace "waiting" to be judged worthy or good enough.

My prayer life has changed. I no longer seek favors. I spend time visualizing the ones I love and thinking positive thoughts about them. I visualize them as happy, healthy, and aware of how much they are loved. I do not believe that Brian's death was part of a divine plan, and I do not believe there was a reason for his death. He did not die so that I would learn how to be a better person. He died because he was born with an undetected birth deformity of his heart. There is no one to blame for this happening.

I met many bereaved parents who never questioned their religious or spiritual beliefs. They never openly expressed feeling anger towards God. At times, I envied their unwavering faith during their journey. The harder I tried to believe as they did, the more conflicted and confused I felt. When I finally stopped trying to force myself to align my beliefs based on what others believed, I was able to find the faith path that was the best for me.

When I think about Brian, I visualize him the way he looked before he died. Handsome, strong, happy. I don't know any other way to visualize him. I can't visualize him as a soul without a physical body. I believe he is someplace where he is happy and free of any physical pain or discomfort. I don't understand but I decided that I did not need understanding, only belief. I do think of him in Heaven because I need to. I need to believe completely that I will see him and be with him again. Belief is my hope, and my hope provides me with the perseverance and resilience to fully embrace my life while I wait for the moment we are reunited.

CHAPTER 14
BE THE KEEPER OF THEIR STORY

We will always remember

BRIAN

Sometime during Brian's funeral my cousin told me that now I need to be the keeper of Brian's story. This became another one of my cherished ways of coping with this loss. John and I would work together to ensure that Brian's life story would not be forgotten. Who he was and what he meant to us and to others will remain alive and remembered with love and happiness.

The first step we took was to establish a yearly scholarship at the University of Nebraska at Lincoln. It was developed to award financial aid to a student who is majoring in the Wildlife Management Program. We are always proud to know that another young adult shares the same passion as Brian, and they learn about his time at the University. We know this scholarship will continue to flourish and grow while benefiting many more students in his memory.

Brian started to play drums when he was 8 years old. He was very active with the Music in the Catholic Schools Program. He loved participating in the percussion section, and we attended many of his concerts. He continued playing during his high school years. He and several of his friends started their own "garage band" and our house was their practice place. They even had a few jobs playing in some of the small local venues. We decided to establish a Memorial Scholarship here as well since his music and drumming career was developed through this program. This scholarship is awarded yearly to a student enrolled in the program to help cover the cost of the program tuition.

Brian did not have many material things other than his drum set and a very old used Suburban. We donated his car to the University so it would be used by the students during their field work. We thought Brian would love this! We read about a clothing drive for high school students that needed clothes for their prom. We donated a few clothing items to this drive and to his former high school for their emergency clothing supply closet. We still have many of his Tshirts which we plan on using to make quilts and pillows for our family.

Brian loved to bird watch. He encouraged us to set up bird feeders in our yard to see what species would visit us. Whenever he came home from the University, he would sit outside on the backyard deck and quietly and patiently wait for the visitors. After his death, John, Brian's Dad built many beautiful wooden bird feeders to share with family and friends. We continue to fill up our feeders and know that Brian would absolutely be thrilled to see how many different birds are visiting.

In one section of our yard, we set up a small memorial garden. We added some ground covers, a few shrubs, mulch and two swings. We would spend many hours in this quiet garden when the grief was fresh and the sadness deep. This is the place where I would feel his presence the most. While sitting quietly on a swing, we can view the birds, enjoy the stillness, and take the time to remember our son. Our memorial garden is simple and does not require much maintenance.

Brian and his dad talked about kayaking on the Omaha area lakes. They never got to reach this goal together, but John was determined to take on this experience in Brian's memory. He researched online and eventually purchased his first kayak.
On Father's Day, we launched on an area lake and discovered a new passion and hobby. I was a bit hesitant on my first try but once I got on the lake I was hooked! We purchased a second kayak and when the weather is cooperating and the wind is not so strong, we visit a lake together in Brian's memory. Being on a lake is also another place where I can feel close to our son. We love the view, the peaceful support of the water and the sounds of the area birds.

One of Brian's friends created a Facebook memorial page where his friends and family posted memories, photos, and remembrances that we could view and appreciate. This page is still available today and I do try to post a comment, meme or photo on his birthday and death anniversary to keep this page active. Social media is a tool that can be used to keep the memory of our child strong. It can be comforting to feel the support and love from others that share in our grief. There are several other social media platforms, but I stay with Facebook because this is the one I am most familiar with.

We keep some of his awards and significant items displayed in our home. We do not see these items as "only things." They provide a connection to Brian through the memories they invoke. Many times, these items and pictures will provide us with the opportunity to talk about their significance to us and how they connect us to Brian. Although we did donate many of his personal items, we never felt that everything of his had to be donated or discarded to show that we progressed in our grief journey.

There are many ways to memorialize a child's life. If the idea of creating and planting a memorial garden sounds perfect, you may choose to set up something in a place that has significance for you. This may be on their school grounds or perhaps a nearby public park where you can add a bench, tree, and flowers. Consider adding a plaque so visitors to the area can appreciate the beautiful space and know that it was created to honor your child.

Support a cause close to their heart or yours through a financial donation or with volunteer hours. Make a tribute donation to a special nonprofit or help with their fundraising events. Perform random simple acts of kindness to honor their life. I met one mother who would pay for another child's birthday cake to honor her child's special day.

Put together small bags of essential daily items to hand out to those seeking assistance in your city. Add a note that mentions how these gifts are your way of sending forth your child's love and their own kindness. Maybe some of their clothing items can be donated to local nonprofits in your community or you can choose to make stuffed animals, blankets, or quilts to keep or decide to share with family and/or friends. If your child had a special hobby they enjoyed or played a musical instrument, consider engaging in that activity for them. Since Brian was a drummer, I found a community drum circle at an area church and for a few months I went there to share his love of drumming. Drumming helped me to feel close to Brian and was a positive way to reduce my stress and anxiety.

Getting a tattoo is a big decision which becomes a permanent reminder of your child that you will always carry with you. There are endless options for a creative meaningful tattoo. You can choose the likeness of your child, a favorite quote, picture, or symbol. You can add their name and a sample of their handwriting. If this is an option you wish to consider, take the time to decide what is most meaningful to you. A search online can provide a vast amount of design suggestions including those specifically designed to memorialize a child. Pinterest is a great online tool to explore designs and gather some ideas.

It is ok to start with something simple and easy to accomplish, especially during the early grief years. Choose what resonates with you the most. You can decide to do things alone, involve family and/or friends, or include a community group traveling on the same journey. You may continue the same activity each year or change what you do as the years go by. Our family gets together each year during his birthday month and death anniversary month. We enjoy a special meal and end the evening with a toast to Brian and the entire family. A candle is always lit to signify his presence is missing.

Regardless of how you chose to honor your child's life story, know that you will be transforming your love into something positive in your child's memory and showing others that love never dies.

CHAPTER 15
MEETING OUR NEEDS WHEN GRIEVING

I know meeting our needs is not top of mind when we are grieving. That is very understandable. However, meeting our needs will support us throughout our grief journey.

Remember we are on a grief journey with many twists and turns and pitstops along the way. Just think of getting on a roller coaster with all the ups and downs. We don't always know ahead of time where the ups and downs will be but being on the roller coaster you would put on the seat belt and use the protective bar to keep you safe and in place. Thinking of our needs ahead of time can support us with the ups and downs and help keep us "safe."

Thinking of our needs ahead of time and making a list of them can be helpful for when we can't think clearly and are exhausted physically and mentally. By making a list of your needs or looking at the following list, you can pick things to do when you are not feeling your best.

Depending where you are on your grief journey or what kind of day you are having will determine which need category is the priority for that day. You can choose how many items you can comfortably do on any given day or week. For example: In the beginning of the grief journey maybe it is just meeting the need of eating food that will give you energy or taking a shower. As the days, months and years go by you can add items and focus on more needs during your days and weeks, making healthy and supportive habits that will support you on the days that are harder for you.

No two individuals will meet their needs in the same way. On the following pages are 8 categories to keep in mind for meeting your needs when on your grief journey. This list is not all inclusive but will cover many of the categories of your needs. You can add more categories or needs to your list that are important for you on your grief journey.

Below each category are ideas of how you can meet your needs in that category. Feel free to brainstorm and add other ways to meet your needs in the below categories.

Mental & Physical Health

* Eating healthy foods that give you energy.

* Drinking your water.

* Be physically active every day. In the beginning it might just be getting up and stretching or going on a 5-minute walk.

* Taking care of your basic hygiene by bathing, brushing your teeth & combing your hair.

* Going to doctor's appointments.

* Going to support groups either virtually or in person.

* Going to therapy appointments.

Mind, Soul & Spirit

* Write down your thoughts/journal.

* Talk to a friend.

* Meditate/Pray

* Do breathing exercises.

* Do yoga.

Social Life & Relationships

* Reach out to friends and family for support. Don't know where to start, look at the cards and messages of people that said contact me if you need anything. Different people can support you in different ways. Example: You have a friend that is good at listening so you can vent to them or maybe another friend loves to cook and can make you a meal.

* Going to a support group with others that "understand" can be a great place to meet people and remain social even if you are just listening in the beginning and not saying a word.

* Share with your close family and friends what you need. For example: Share with them if you need more alone time, want to celebrate the holidays in a different way, how you want to observe the birthday and anniversary dates or if you need more support from them in some way.

Leisure Time/Rest

* Have balance in your life by resting when you need to.

* Plan time to just "do nothing."

* Make time to do something you enjoy. This might feel hard at first, so one idea would be to do something in memory of your child or loved one and remember them and honor their memory when participating in the activity.

Home Environment

This might be an area where you ask for help from others or pay for services that you don't normally use.

* Go online and buy your groceries and have them delivered.

* Go online and buy whatever you need to buy so you don't have to go inside a store if you are not feeling up to it.

* Ask for someone to help or pay someone to do the dishes, laundry, and cleaning in your home. I remember after my son, Diego died, I had a few friends some to my house here and there and clean in my home. This was very helpful because I didn't have the energy emotionally or physically to clean, etc. *This might be a great thing to ask people when you don't know what to ask from those that said, "Call me if you need anything." Or if you are reading this and know someone that is grieving this might be a great thing to ask if they need help with: cleaning, laundry, food, etc.*

Growth

I listed this category as growth which can mean many things for different people depending on where you are on your grief journey.

* Read books, watch documentaries, etc. that are about the topic of grief, other people's stories and being on a grief journey.

* Go to support groups and as time goes by you can give back by sharing your grief journey with others or presenting a topic that will help others on their grief journey.

* Build positive and healthy routines/habits that will support you on your grief journey. For support ask a friend or work with a coach.

* Share your story with others. There are many ways to do this: on social media, a website, by writing a blog or book, at a support group or by speaking at an organization or business.

Creativity

* Honor your child or loved one's memory by doing something creative such as having an event in their memory, donating in their name or to an important cause. *Donating can be to an organization or paying it forward by buying a birthday cake or paying for someone else's meal at a restaurant.*

* Making a website/social media page or posting in memory of your child or loved one.

Financial

Financial needs can be very different for many people. I have added this need category to the list because finances can add a lot of extra stress. When grieving it is very possible that we worked less, are making less money, are not opening the mail so then we don't pay the bills on time, or we just don't have the money to pay them due to all the extra expenses related to the death.

* At least monthly look at your finances. If you can't do it ask a trusted family or friend to help you.

* If money is tight, reach out to family, friends, a religious organization, or other helping organizations and ask for help. I know this can be hard to do, but there are many people that want to help. They won't know you need help if you don't ask.

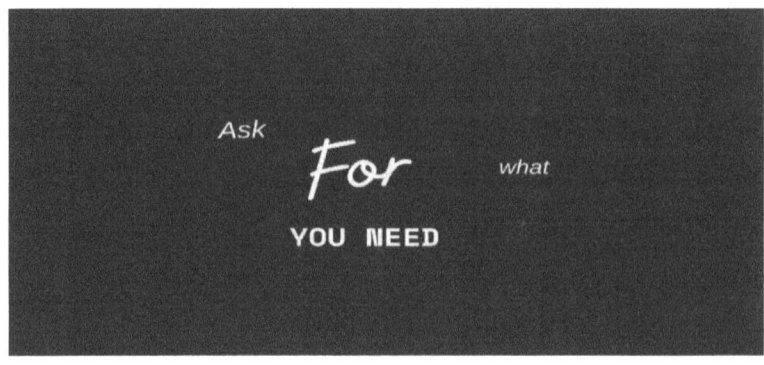

CHAPTER 16
MEMORIES SHARED BY LOVED ONES

Thank you to those of you who shared your memories for this book or just privately with us. For a bereaved parent we love it when you remember our children and the memories.

Don't be afraid to say their name or to share a memory that you have. I know sometimes you may be afraid of sharing because you think you will make the bereaved parent "sad." This is not true. You are not making us sad, you are sharing and partaking in remembering our children. We can have and experience so many different emotions: sad, happy, angry and the list can go on and on. So many different emotions when we are on this grief journey.

Please remember our children and say their names.

THE GRIEF JOURNEY WHEN A CHILD DIES

MEMORIES SHARED BY DIEGO'S LOVED ONES

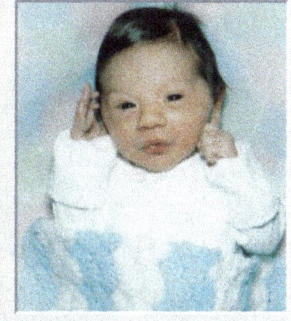

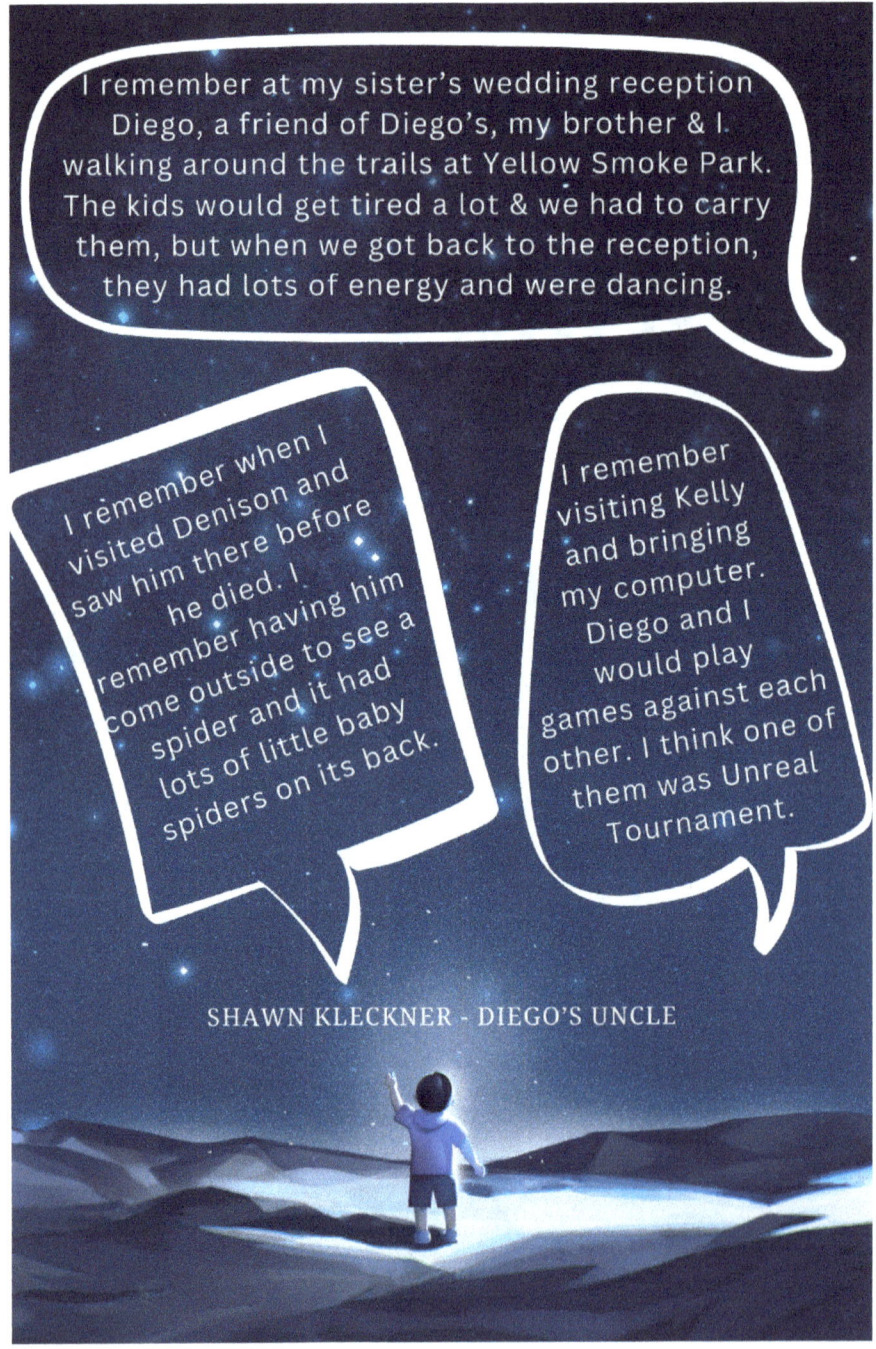

So many memories of Diego. His sweet smiling face could often be seen in our office with his mom, Kelly. Always wanting to help. He used to love to help me fold letters and stuff envelopes. We would talk about soccer, food, his sister, and more soccer. He'd check my desk to see if I had any snacks. Always on-the-go and full of energy. Diego was such a funny and loving boy. A sweet boy that loved his family, friends and soccer.
A sweet soul taken way too soon.

Denise Tiemens

I think this memory may have been in the summer of 2003 when Diego spent some time on the farm.

We had a little shed down south where my buildings are now, and we would take goats down there for summer pasture. I would need to go down there to take care of them each day, like watering. Diego followed me around, and he liked to go down there because there was this big, aggressive Nubian buck. He would like to go on the back of the buck like how the cowboys do bull riding at the rodeo. I think I would help him get on his back. He had a lot of fun with that goat. He would call him Rodeo.

Lance Kleckner, Diego's Uncle

A good picture of the sky and Diego's tree.
I planted the tree on August 26, 2004. When the girls came here for their first summer in 2010, it fell because root girdled a part of the trunk, so kind of died like Diego.
I replanted a princeton elm in 2011 in the same place, so Diego's tree lives on and I think of him when I see it.

Lance Kleckner, Diego's Uncle

We had a few ferrets. They liked to bite, so Diego was scared of them. When he spent time here, I taught him how to grab and hold them and he wasn't scared of them anymore.

Lance Kleckner
Diego's Uncle

Diego's Last Adventure

It was late June of 2004 that Diego visited our family farm near Denison Iowa. When he came to the farm, I asked how long was he going to stay, 1 week? 2 weeks? I joked. No, he said 'All summer'. Shortly after he was here, my brother & his uncle, Shawn visited, as he came often during the summer months. So soon we were all off to what we thought would be our first adventure of the summer.

We started walking up and down hills, but eventually we got to a creek and continued to follow that. Shawn and Diego didn't mind walking in the creek, but I didn't want to get my newer shoes wet, so I followed them on the side of the creek. As we continued, this creek joined a larger one. Eventually, I would have to walk in the water to cross the creek. Now when we would cross the deeper creek, I would put Diego on my back.

There were rocks all over, so we looked through them. Diego picked a couple rocks he wanted to take back with him. I grabbed a large, circular, narrow, blackish rock, and Diego thought that one was interesting and that I should take it back.

Eventually it was annoying to walk around with a big rock, so I 'accidentally' dropped it, and it broke as it was a more fragile rock. We eventually decided to go back, and since home was miles away now, Diego would piggyback on me some of the way as he was tired now. It didn't take too long to get home and once we were home; he wasn't too tired to go see the kittens in the barn. I kept the two rocks that he picked out to remember our last adventure together.

The two rocks Diego picked out on his last adventure.

Lance Kleckner, Diego's Uncle

Even though we are reaching the 20th year anniversary of Diego's passing, the memories I have feel like yesterday. I remember sitting with him most mornings before class started in elementary school. I loved when he would bring in a Honey Bun and share without me even asking. We would each pull apart a piece of the pastry while giggling and talking about how much we loved soccer.

I also vividly remember when Diego passed. I felt confused on where my friend went and why he wasn't coming back to school from the hospital. I cried in my mom's arms after learning that he was now with Jesus. The mornings before school felt empty. I have since ran into Kelly over the years and in those moments it takes me back to seeing Diego's big smile holding our favorite snack.

Mia (Blackman) Paesl
Classmate of Diego's

Diego was this cute child who was energetic, loved soccer, and never knew a stranger. Diego's death was devastating to all of us.

As a pediatric nurse, I had been concerned that young children were not allowed to go to funerals and visitations. Children are big thinkers and understand much more than we give them credit for.

One thing that impressed me so much was Diego's friends that came to the visitation and the funeral. The children brought pictures and articles that they related to Diego. They honored him and immortalized him in their own way. I knew they would carry on the dreams that they had talked about with Diego.

Carol Timm

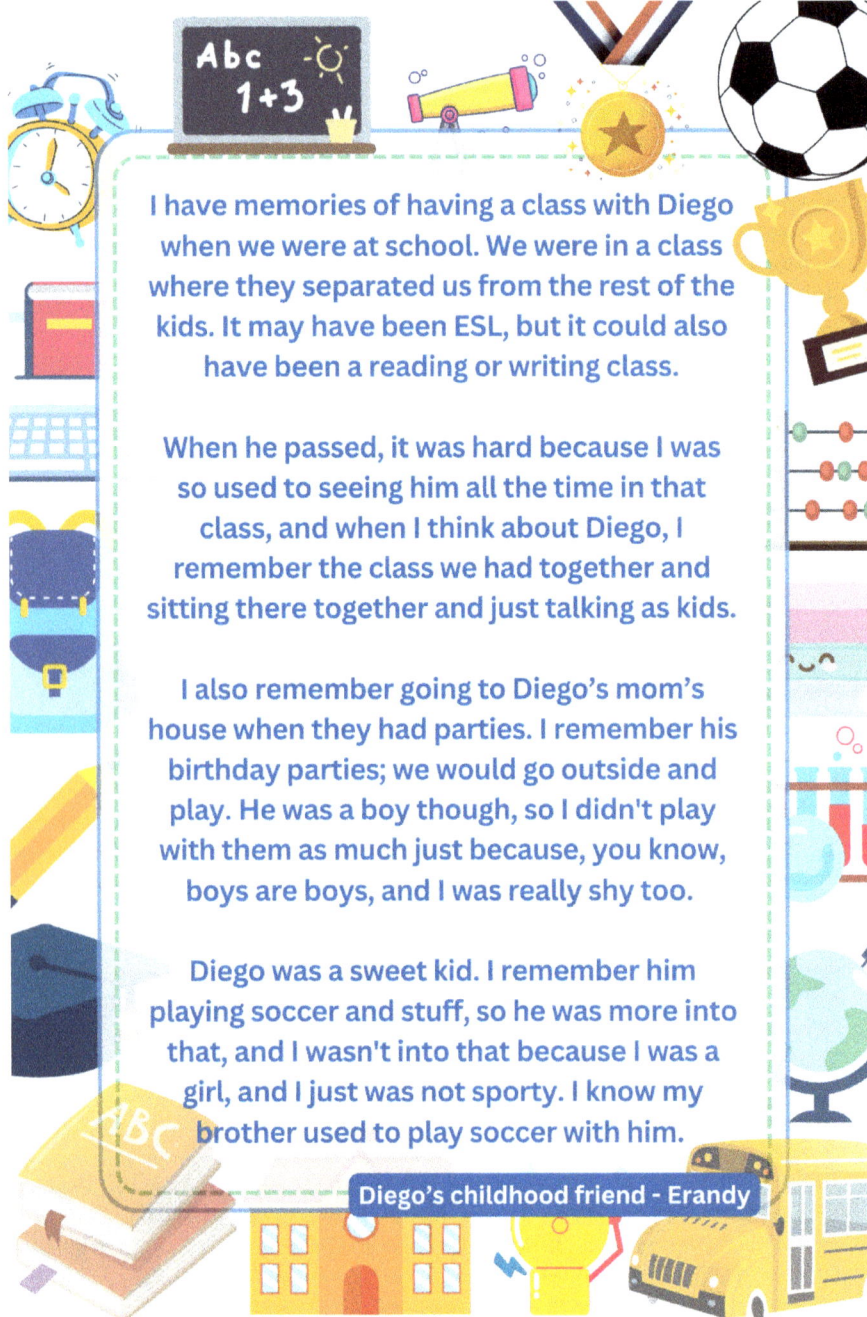

I have memories of having a class with Diego when we were at school. We were in a class where they separated us from the rest of the kids. It may have been ESL, but it could also have been a reading or writing class.

When he passed, it was hard because I was so used to seeing him all the time in that class, and when I think about Diego, I remember the class we had together and sitting there together and just talking as kids.

I also remember going to Diego's mom's house when they had parties. I remember his birthday parties; we would go outside and play. He was a boy though, so I didn't play with them as much just because, you know, boys are boys, and I was really shy too.

Diego was a sweet kid. I remember him playing soccer and stuff, so he was more into that, and I wasn't into that because I was a girl, and I just was not sporty. I know my brother used to play soccer with him.

Diego's childhood friend - Erandy

I remember when he passed away because my mom called me into her room and sat me down to tell me. it was a little hard for me to understand, of course, because I was a little kid. I didn't know what it meant when someone would pass away and I remember not understanding, but I remember being sad because I knew what it meant, but I didn't fully understand.

I asked my mom what happened to him, and she told me what we thought we knew had happened at the time. She probably didn't want to give me details because I was so little, but I remember asking her what happened to him, and she told me. She told me, but we didn't know why, and she just told me, she's like I don't know what happened.

Diego's childhood friend - Erandy

I remember the funeral home.
I wasn't allowed to go inside, so I remember sitting outside and not going in because my mom didn't let me. I saw Diego's family there and I was still trying to comprehend what happened.

The moments that it really hit me was when I would go to school. I'd go into that class, and he wasn't there.

The teacher was telling me it's going to be okay. It felt weird because he wasn't there anymore, and so I remember, mainly him being gone.

Diego's childhood friend - Erandy

The Parties

When Diego's mom would throw parties with the girls, and to the parties I've been to, every time I would go to Diego's house and every time, I'm at the parties all I would think about is Diego is not here, you know, he is missing. It's like something is missing.
It didn't feel right.

You could feel that he was gone, and he was missed.

When Diego's mom had his other sisters' parties, I would go to the parties and still look around, like am I going to see Diego? Like I'm going to see him playing outside.

Diego's childhood friend - Erandy

I think that is how grief is: you forget someone, not that you forget, but you live your day-to-day life and then realize that person is gone.

Like with my cousin Diego (I had my friend Diego, and a cousin named Diego, also.) when he passed, I feel like he's still with us, but he is just doing his own thing. That he is out there somewhere, and then it really hits you that he is not here. When you're around family, and he should be there, and he's not there, it feels empty. It doesn't feel whole.

So, with Diego passing, he was the first person that passed in my life that I was close to. I haven't lost a lot of people in my life. It has been mainly him and my cousin Diego that have passed. Their anniversary dates of them passing are only two days of a difference (of different years.) When Diego's anniversary comes up, I think of my cousin and vice versa.

Every time I see a picture that Diego's mom shares of him, I remember him. I remember his big smile and his energetic self. It is all visual, so it's all in my head. I try to put it into words. He was always such a great kid. He was always a sweet, energetic kid, for sure.

Diego's childhood friend - Erandy

"I still remember him coming to my parties and wearing this distinct shirt, it was a button up and had like a low rider on it. He said it was his favorite. Lol. Very random memory but makes me smile remembering how proud he was of that shirt."

Diego's childhood friend - Jonathan

There was a party at my aunt's house. I remember asking my mom if Diego was going to come there. He was my only friend so I figured I'd ask not knowing if you all even knew my aunt. My mom said he might be.

You guys never came and the next day my mom got the call and was informed Diego had passed away. I still remember hearing my mom yell and I knew something was wrong, but she wouldn't tell me until she got off the phone. All this time has passed, and I'll never forget that moment. That was the first time I dealt with a loss of someone I cared for.

Diego's childhood friend - Jonathan

MEMORIES SHARED BY BRIAN'S LOVED ONES

A Father's Memories

My first favorite memory involves a lawnmower. Brian was old enough to learn how to drive but still young enough to not consider this as an actual boring job responsibility. We had an old lawn tractor and a full acre of grass to mow. He was happy to take on this task once I pointed out to him how this will help him learn how to drive. He enjoyed the work as he was able to drive the tractor independently, but in the spring time we would have an influx of barn swallows that evidently had a nest in one of our trees. They would dive down towards his head while he was mowing. They never actually touched him but they obviously saw him as a threat to their nest. We would stand at the kitchen window laughing while watching him maneuver the tractor in all different directions to get away from the birds. He would come back into the house showing his extreme frustration in trying to get the job done without the bird's interference. I always thought it was interesting that later in his life he became a true bird lover!

Brian always loved being outdoors and longed to participate in my yearly hunting trips to Nebraska National Forest located outside of Halsey. He was probably around 10 or 11 years old when he was finally able to tag along. On that first trip, the weather was cold with about a foot of snow. These were ideal conditions for tracking deer. He was interested in following the deer tracks as we hiked our way through the forest. He was especially excited when those deer tracks led him to a gut pile. He wasn't so interested in seeing the deer as much as he was interested in finding those remains. Needless to say, our trip ended without a deer to bring home but we did return with plenty of good memories.

John, Brian's Father

A Sister's Memories

The night Brian died, he had called home. I answered the phone & he told me about everything he was doing in Puerto Rico. He told me about all the food they were eating & their time in the jungle. He was catching small lizards & having them hang on his ear lobe. I remember telling him to make sure he took a picture because I wanted to see that! I was invited out for a friend's birthday party that night but decided to stay home and work on homework. When I think about that phone call, I'm always thankful I stayed home that night & was able to have that conversation with him.

When Brian & I were both home one day in high school, I had just broken up with a boyfriend and was crying at the kitchen table. He came into the kitchen and put his hand on my shoulder and told me it would be ok.

Another one of my favorite memories with Brian was when we were both in grade school. It had just snowed & we went with our Dad to his friend's house. He had us all suited up in all of our snow pants, boots and gloves. When we got to his friend's house, we got to go outside and play with his 2 Weimaraner dogs in the snow. Brian & I just ran around the backyard with these 2 big dogs chasing us & knocking us over in all of the snow.

Molly, Brian's Sister

Brian was the son, brother, and uncle I can only aspire to be. Family was first and foremost to him, whether it was hanging out at the nursing home with Grandma Ann or taking time out of his college life to show his niece and nephew around the Lincoln Children's Zoo. The greatest sorrow I feel in this tragedy is for three little kids who've lost the best uncle they'll ever know. Brian took great joy in being an uncle to Connor, Cassidy and Olivia and they absolutely adored him. He delighted in traipsing around in the field behind our parents' house, with Connor, Cassidy and Olivia in tow, looking for bunnies and snakes and pointing out the different plants and insects. One such outing resulted in the foursome coming back covered in chigger bites- I think Brian ended up with the worst of it. In typical Brian fashion he had several treatment methods for us within a day. One of the highlights of any visit with Uncle Brian was wrestling with him. And when he wasn't rolling around on the ground, playing with them like a kid himself, he was taking time to share his knowledge of nature with them. As deeply as it pains me to think of all the great time spent with Brain that they are now deprived of, I will do everything in my ability to help them treasure the time they did have with him.

Mike, Brian and Lisa
Brian's Brother & Sister-in-Law

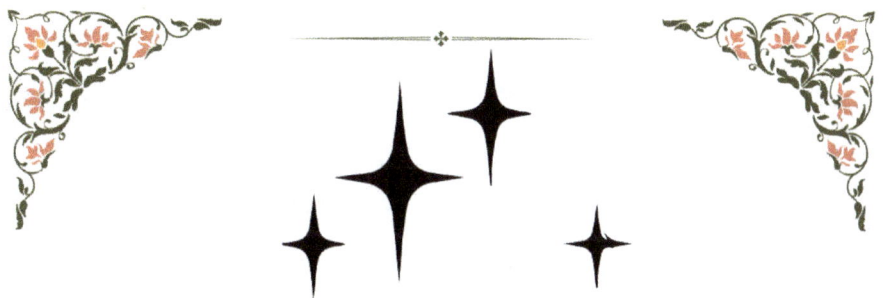

I was around 23 years old when Brian was about 8 years old. My friend Dave died in an airplane crash. When I came home from Florida for a visit, Brian gave me a wood carved figure. He told me it was to take away the bad dreams and that I could have it to help me deal with Dave's death. He didn't want me to have bad dreams about my friend. After giving me the figure, I only had good dreams of Dave. I still have the figure in my room. Everytime I look at it, I think of Brian and his amazing compassion and empathy at such a young age.

Molly and Heather (Brian's sisters) and Brian

Who Would Have Known

Who would have known
Such a shy little kid
Would grow up to be such
An outgoing young man

Who would have guessed
That worried little boy in search of perfection
Would dazzle everyone around him
With such passionate worldly ventures

Who would ever imagine
This quiet individual
Would impress us all
As a witty and eloquent speaker

Who could predict
How those early years would mold you
Into this wonderful human being
Who would profoundly touch our lives forever

Who would have known
That as an uncle so young
You had already helped us mold
The generation to come

Who could have guessed
That all the plans we had
And relationship we hoped to strengthen
Would only be dreams never fulfilled

If we had only known
We would have told you
How much you were loved
And extremely admired

We should have told you the joy we felt
Every time you hugged our children,
Shared your wisdom,
Or simply showed an interest

We should have told you how proud we were
That you cared so much for others,
Followed your dreams,
And placed us as a priority

Who would have known....
Oh how I wish we had known!

All My Love
Lisa, Brian's Sister-in-Law

CHAPTER 17
REMEMBERING OUR CHILDREN

Thank you to those that are sharing their children with us here in our book or privately with us. Remembering our children is important for our grief journey.

Aidan
You are missed so much by so many people.
Your infectious smile, your laugh, your love of animals, your love for our country and the love for your family and friends. I miss you every second of every day. I love you a bushel and a peck and a hug around the neck...
forever and always...pinky promise.
Love,
Mommy

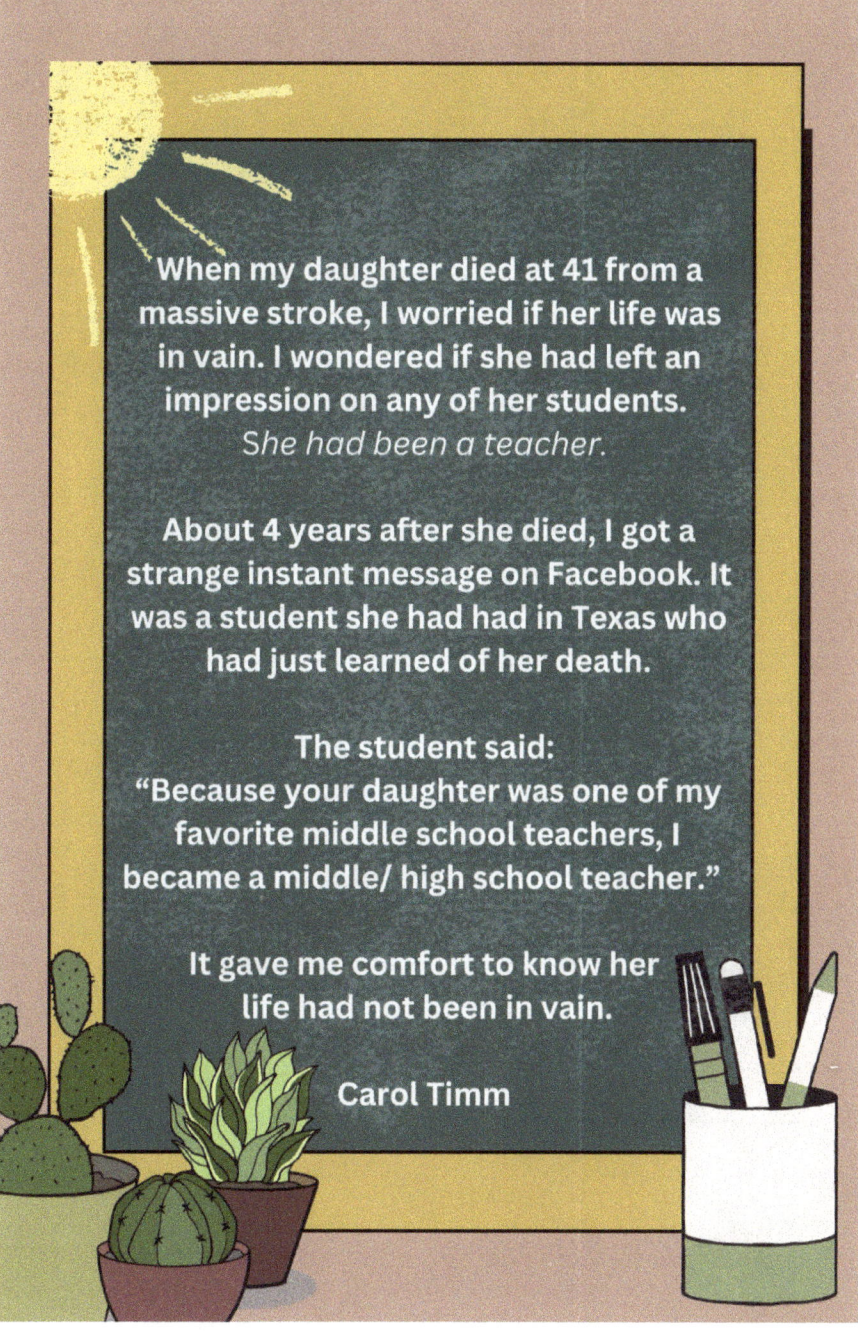

When my daughter died at 41 from a massive stroke, I worried if her life was in vain. I wondered if she had left an impression on any of her students.
She had been a teacher.

About 4 years after she died, I got a strange instant message on Facebook. It was a student she had had in Texas who had just learned of her death.

The student said:
"Because your daughter was one of my favorite middle school teachers, I became a middle/ high school teacher."

It gave me comfort to know her life had not been in vain.

Carol Timm

William Carl Drieling
Forever Loved

Two years after William died, my Bennington house was being shingled. A worker slammed a pack of shingles on my kitchen roof area and I heard a noise of something falling. My heart coffee cup landed upside down in my kitchen sink without breaking! This was also the same year (2010) his beautiful head stone was placed at his grave.

Beth Pribil - William's Mom

CHAPTER 18
FINDING YOUR GRIEF SUPPORT

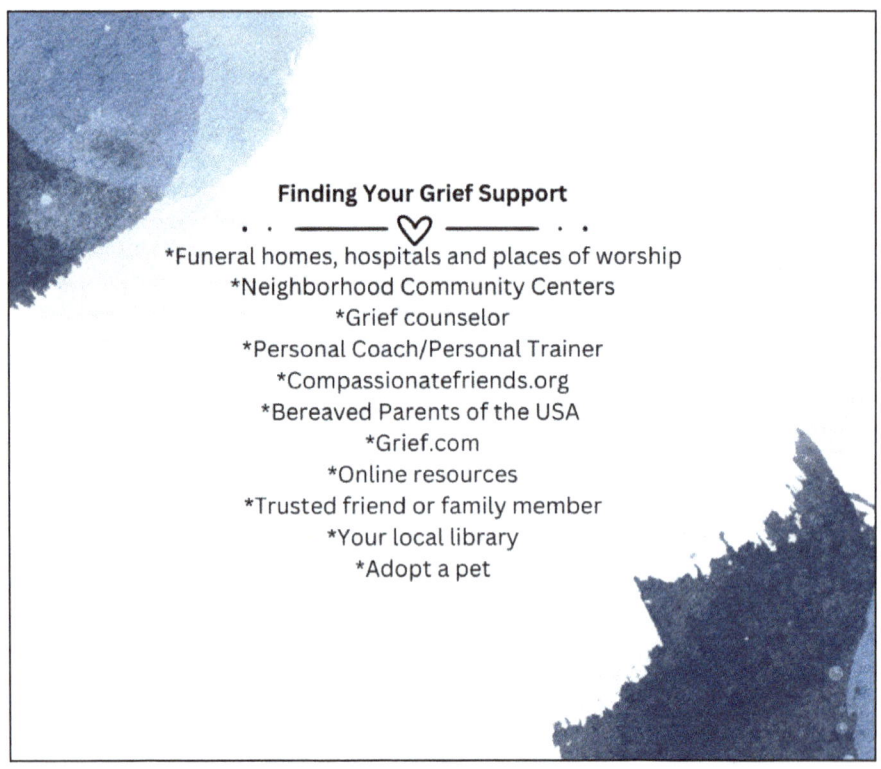

Finding Your Grief Support

*Funeral homes, hospitals and places of worship
*Neighborhood Community Centers
*Grief counselor
*Personal Coach/Personal Trainer
*Compassionatefriends.org
*Bereaved Parents of the USA
*Grief.com
*Online resources
*Trusted friend or family member
*Your local library
*Adopt a pet

Just like the unique personality of your child and the circumstances of the loss, you will handle your grief in your own personal way. Not every parent wishes to talk and share openly in a support group. Some parents may lean on their faith and others may question their beliefs and feel isolated from God, their religion, and their church. Not every parent will find journal writing soothing while others may value writing down their personal feelings and emotions. This chapter is included to provide a brief review of some of the options that can be considered if you feel ready to find additional support. The tools we list can be added to your grief toolbox for a short time or they may remain with you as your primary coping strategies for many months or even years.

Finding a support group that resonates with you may take some time and effort and their focus of support may be different. Funeral homes, hospitals, and places of worship frequently offer support groups that provide grief education and a variety of coping resources and suggestions. Check your neighborhood community centers as

well. It may be helpful to simply be with other people that are also experiencing a life-changing loss. Learning that you are not alone on your journey can help you realize that everything you are experiencing is very normal and your challenges, feelings and emotions are all part of deep grief. This knowledge alone can provide a small measure of relief and comfort.

The Compassionate Friends is a non-profit self-help organization with over 600 chapters serving all 50 states and 30 countries. Their mission is to provide understanding and hope to bereaved families experiencing the death of a child, grandchild, and/or sibling. The local chapters generally hold monthly meetings where stories are shared, and support is provided. Attendance and topics will vary at each meeting and all meetings are led by volunteers who are further out on their journey. You can search on Compassionatefriends.org website to find a local chapter and review their extensive list of resources. They also offer 24/7 private Facebook groups, crisis hotline information, an online magazine, and a list of related organizations.

Some local chapters may still offer virtual chapter meetings via Zoom and an Online Support Community for live chats. All these options are designed to provide confidential, non-judgmental support and encouragement. You can also request grief resource materials that can address your specific situation. There are many other additional online resources available to review if attending an in-person meeting is not an option you are comfortable with or feel ready for. The Bereaved Parents of the USA, Grief.com and Hospicefoundation.org are just 3 of the available online support options. You can easily search for additional websites that may also be geared toward a specific cause of death.

If a group setting is not something you feel is right for you, consider finding a grief counselor for individual sessions. Your loss will affect every aspect of your personal and family life and perhaps it will impact your work performance. You may acknowledge those aspects but not feel comfortable sharing in a group setting. Many workplaces now offer counseling services as part of their benefit packages and may cover some or all the costs included. Check with your Human Resources Department to ask about such benefits and if they can provide recommendations.

The grief we experience can cause tremendous stress which will often negatively impact our physical health. If you feel ready to include some form of exercise or physical activity, working with a Personal Coach or Personal Trainer can be beneficial. They can help develop and initiate a wellness or activity plan and provide feedback on overcoming obstacles. Working with a coach and focusing on a fitness plan can help provide a reprieve from focusing only on your grief and encourage you to care for your physical self. To find a certified professional, check with your workplace Human Resources Department, local gyms/fitness facilities, your insurance company, or ask your physician, friends, and family for recommendations. For credentialed coaches you may search the International Coaching Federation or the National Board for Health and Wellness Coaching websites.

If you find that reading on your own is the best option for you, there are plenty of books available on grief and specifically on the loss of a child. Visit your local library, search Amazon, or review the suggested books on a grief website.

Finding a trusted family member or friend that is willing to spend time with you can be a tremendous support. This is the person that will listen without judgment and let you express all your feelings, emotions, fears, and struggles. The most supportive person may or may not have experienced the loss of a child, but they are

compassionate and empathetic. You may connect with someone you meet online or at an in-person grief support group. Be open to new people coming into your life that can offer such companionship and support.

One final suggestion: if you feel ready to take on the responsibility, consider adopting a pet. There are many animal rescue groups that would love to help with choosing the right pet to match your needs and lifestyle. Grieving can be lonely, and we may often find ourselves isolated at home. A dog or cat can become the perfect companion who will provide unconditional love, attention, and acceptance without judgment. Interacting with a pet can help to increase your physical activity and encourage some much-needed respite from your grief journey.

CHAPTER 19
FOR OUR SUPPORTERS

Maybe you are reading this because you have a friend, co-worker or family member living with the loss of their child or grandchild. Maybe you are searching for the best way to offer support and walk alongside this person. This is the group that no one wishes to be a part of and providing support can sometimes be challenging. We will all grieve differently and often wish that others understood that our grief journey will be unique to us. One parent may want to be alone while another may need someone close by. Sometimes what we need and want for support may change. Everyday can be different for us.

Just know that we may want to talk about our child very much, just like all parents and grandparents do. If talking is what we need, please let us talk! Don't worry that we may get sad and become tearful. Those tears are a sign of tremendous love. They are a huge part of the awful process of deep grief. We are not able to always control the tears; they come when they need to. Be committed to listening without judgment. Offer us a listening ear, a hug, and be a comforting presence nearby which may be exactly what we need. It is not necessary to tell us our child would not want us to be sad. It is appropriate for sadness to exist alongside love until we find our way. I believe our loved one is with us, understands, supports, and encourages us.

Let us share the memories we have, even when we may be sharing the same memories again and again. We are acutely aware of how there will be no new memories made. The ones we have sustain us. Our lives have been shattered when our child died. It takes time to put those torn pieces of our lives and ourselves back together. Many pieces will no longer fit, but we will need to find our own way of keeping those memories with us.

Please say their name! It is heavenly music for us, and we love to know that others remember. Reach out in some way as birthday, holidays, or special anniversary dates approach. Send flowers, a card, note or even a text message. We will treasure knowing that our child is remembered and that others acknowledge the undesired road we are traveling on. I still remember a card received from a friend on the first Christmas. The card acknowledged the approaching holiday but also spoke to the inevitable grief I would experience during the holiday season.

Please forgive us if we find ourselves unable to attend a family event, holiday gathering or any other special occasion. Although we want and appreciate family support, it can be incredibly painful to see our family gathered without our much-loved child there with us. It is a common belief that the first year of loss is the hardest as we face the first anniversary, birthday, or holiday. And they are hard, but the next year or subsequent years can be painful as well. The shock and numbness will lessen, and we will be looking at a future with an entirely different picture of what we anticipated for ourselves, our family, and our child.

Most of all, please be patient with us. The journey we were forced to travel went directly through the center of hell. That road can't be traveled without deep sorrow, confusion, turmoil, and massive changes. As we find and navigate our way through in our own time, we will be different people. Never the same. Forever changed, forever missing our child but always grateful for every heartfelt gesture of support.

For our supporters written by:
Brian's Mom, JoAnn

THE GRIEF JOURNEY WHEN A CHILD DIES

ABOUT THE AUTHORS

ABOUT THE AUTHOR
KELLY KLECKNER

Kelly has supported many grieving parents, adults, and children when on their grieving journeys. She has done this through her past work in the social service non-profit field, as a volunteer for the Omaha Chapter of Compassionate Friends and by coaching people on their grief journeys as a Life and Wellness Coach & Parent Coach.

At the time of initial publication of this book, Kelly had 4 children and one granddaughter. She has 3 daughters and had a son, Diego who died in June of 2004 at the age of 8 years old. She is an animal lover and currently has 2 dogs and 2 cats.

Kelly loves to stay busy by pursuing her passion of helping others by coaching and her volunteer work. Kelly also enjoys watching comedy movies, spending time with her family & pets, and having connection chats with her friends, peers, and new acquaintances. For information and updates about what Kelly is doing go to her website: www.kellykleckner.com.

AUTHOR KELLY KLECKNER

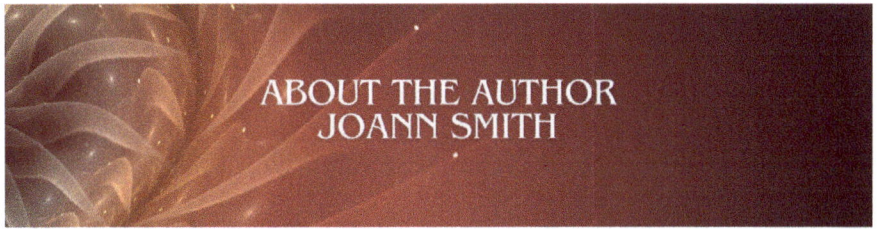

ABOUT THE AUTHOR
JOANN SMITH

JoAnn relocated to Nebraska from New Jersey to teach for Omaha Public Schools. However, teaching in the fitness and wellness field has always been a part of her life. After sustaining a back injury, she recovered by focusing on a consistent Pilates practice. Her practice became even more meaningful after her son Brian died from an undiagnosed heart condition in March of 2008.

JoAnn continues to teach in her son's memory at the Pilates Center of Omaha and is thrilled to teach her two nieces each week via Zoom. She was honored to see her story about Brian and her Pilates practice shared in the December 2017 issue of PilatesStyle magazine.

When not teaching, she loves to kayak with her husband, walk with friends, and spend time with her grandchildren and blended family which includes Mike, Heather, Molly, and Brian. They are now the happy owners of Bob Barker, a two-year-old boxer mix adopted from the local Humane Society. Bob keeps them both active and busy.

AUTHOR JOANN SMITH

www.ingramcontent.com/pod-product-compliance
Lightning Source LLC
Chambersburg PA
CBHW060133100426
42744CB00007B/775